"THE FOOT OF JESUS"

YESUPADAM

REACHING INDIA'S "UNTOUCHED"

Terri Whitaker

BELIEVE BOOKS
Life Stories That Inspire
WASHINGTON, DC

YESUPADAM
By Terri Whitaker

Unless otherwise noted, all Scripture quotations are from the HOLY BIBLE, KING JAMES VERSION (KJV).

Scripture quotations identified as NASB are taken from the NEW AMERICAN STANDARD BIBLE ®, Copyright © 1960, 1962, 1963, 1968, 1971, 1972, 1973, 1975, 1977, 1995 by The Lockman Foundation. Used by permission.

Scripture quotations identified as NKJV are taken from the New King James Version. Copyright © 1982 by Thomas Nelson, Inc. Used by permission. All rights reserved.

Scripture quotations identified as NIV are taken from the HOLY BIBLE, NEW INTERNATIONAL VERSION ®. Copyright © 1973, 1978, 1984 International Bible Society. Used by permission of Zondervan. All rights reserved.

Scripture quotations identified as TNIV are taken from the HOLY BIBLE, TODAY'S NEW INTERNATIONAL VERSION ®. Copyright © 2001, 2005 by International Bible Society ®. Used by permission of International Bible Society ®. All rights reserved worldwide.

"NIV," "NEW INTERNATIONAL VERSION," "TNIV," and "TODAY'S NEW INTERNATIONAL VERSION" are trademarks registered in the United States Patent and Trademark Office by International Bible Society ®. Use of each trademark requires the permission of International Bible Society.

ISBN: 0-9787428-3-4

Library of Congress Control Number: 2007935125

Cover design: *Jack Kotowicz, Washington, DC, VelocityDesignGroup.com*
Layout design: *Annie Kotowicz*

Believe Books publishes the inspirational life stories of extraordinary believers in God from around the world. Requests for information should be addressed to **Believe Books** at www.believebooks.com. **Believe Books** is a registered trade name of **Believe Books, LLC** of Washington, DC.

Printed in the United States of America

For my father,
whose passion for India
gave life to this book

Your faith presses me into
a deeper trust in our mighty God

CONTENTS

ACKNOWLEDGEMENTS

I would like to express my deep thanks and appreciation to the many people who have made this project possible.

Dianne and Annie, your edits, encouragements, and especially your prayers were of such a help to me throughout the publishing process. Your godward orientation even in the details of getting this to press made this process a joy.

Jack, thank you for your skillful design work. You bring the essence of India to the cover.

To the team at the Piquant Agency, thank you for taking this book on and working so hard with me to find an outlet for this story.

Not only my appreciation, but my admiration and respect goes to the myriad of pastors and staff at Love-n-Care Ministries: Your zeal for God's kingdom is the reason for this book, and your simple and sure faith is beautiful to see. May God only increase your love and fruitfulness.

Monika and Yesupadam, thank you for being patient with me as I barraged you with questions and asked for large chunks out of your very busy schedules. Your friendship and example has been a great blessing to me.

To my mother, who is now in the presence of the Lord, I owe more than I can say. She encouraged me in my writing from childhood, and made many sacrifices in order to allow me the opportunity to write this book. More, her commitment to God and His kingdom has shaped my life immeasurably. I love and miss you, Mom.

Dad, you were the one who gave me the vision to write this book. You sent me to India even when funds were scarce, and your faith encouraged me to keep going when I got discouraged. You have the kind of faith in God that gets stronger as circumstances get tougher, and I admire that so much.

My greatest debt goes to my wonderful husband Vance, who supported me in the daily responsibility of writing, prayed with me, had faith for me when I was weak, and challenged me to believe in a God who is greater than my weaknesses. You patiently labored over every word in this book and offered invaluable insight. I count your love, friendship, and insight into my life as my greatest earthly gift.

PREFACE

India is an ancient place, a nation steeped in culture, history, and tradition. It is a country that is proud of its heritage and its people. There is much to celebrate in the beauty of India—a land full of colors, spices, literature, and history. But while some of India's traditions give it a delightful character, other cultural laws have suffocated justice and mercy. Some of the injustices of Indian society have oppressed whole classes of people, and many of the people in this book have been directly affected by caste prejudice and cultural taboos. A closer look at these structures in Indian society is key to understanding the life of Yesupadam and those around him.

The caste system is a crucial part of the Indian way of life. Instituted over 1,500 years ago, the caste system provides structure to Hindu society. It is a social system that finds its meaning in Hinduism. Legend has it that one of the gods created man from his body: the Brahmins (the priests) came from his head, the Kshatriyas (the warriors) came from his arms, the Vaisyas (the merchants and tradesmen) from his legs, and the Sudras (laborers) from his feet. These four main groupings contain hundreds of castes and subcastes.[1]

Outside of these, however, are the untouchables. Excluded from the caste system, they are the "outcastes," the lowest of the low, the outsiders. Hindus consider those outside the caste system to be unclean because they do not descend from a divine being, and many Hindus will literally refuse to make any physical contact with an untouchable. Untouchables represent 300 million of India's billion-strong population—about 30 percent of the nation.

These millions are the accursed of Hindu society. Little wonder that these outsiders to the caste system have labeled themselves "Dalits," which means "oppressed."

To make matters more difficult, caste status is hereditary, so those born Dalits are doomed to remain Dalits for life, and they pass on that status to their children. The caste system is closely linked to the Hindu belief in reincarnation; because a person earns his status in the next life on the basis of his behavior in the previous life, an untouchable is someone who achieved that low status on the basis of actions. Thus, the caste system eats away at the basic equality of mankind. In the Hindu conception of the world, inequality is assumed. People are born unequal, not out of injustice, but simply because they deserve it.

This ancient system of caste, deeply embedded in Indian society, brings with it many traditions and habits. Untouchables usually perform the lowest jobs in any community—cleaning out sewers and latrines by hand, burying or cremating the dead, handling blood and bodily fluids, and whatever else is defiling according to Hindu law. They become doubly filthy in the eyes of a devout Hindu. Even those untouchables who perform acceptable jobs such as farming and day laboring, however, carry the stigma of being unclean. Because of their status, Dalits are not allowed in Hindu temples, although the vast majority of them practice that faith. Out of necessity, many untouchable communities build their own Dalit temples and appoint Dalit priests, so that they can continue to be faithful to the religion that has oppressed them.

Fortunately, modern Indian law has outlawed discrimination on the basis of caste, and has even abolished untouchability. Unfortunately, the application and enforcement of these laws are sporadic at best. In many urban areas, people have begun to move beyond the limits of caste, and occasionally untouchables will even marry into high-caste families. Thus, progress is being made in some places. In rural communities, however, the caste system has more power, and it is more difficult to overcome. Since more than three-quarters of Indians live in rural areas, the injustices of caste discrimination live on.

Indian legislators have taken steps to try to create equal opportunities for Dalits, and these efforts have resulted in something comparable to "affirmative action" in the U.S. There are scholarships, endowments, grants, and reserved places for untouchables in many Indian universities. Through education, untouchables are encouraged to enter career paths formerly reserved for higher-caste Indians. In fact, nearly 25 percent of government jobs and college seats have been reserved for untouchables, opening up unprecedented opportunities for Dalits.[2]

Christian untouchables, however, are excluded from such benefits. Even in the midst of attempts to eliminate caste prejudice, religious prejudice continues unabated. Impossible as it may sound, an untouchable is eligible for government aid as long as he is any religion other than Christian or Muslim. Only Christians and Muslims are excluded from government scholarships and grants.[3] An untouchable can be Hindu, Buddhist, Sikh, or Jain, but conversion to Christianity automatically excludes him from governmental benefits. In theory, this is because religions like Christianity lack a caste system, and so caste discrimination has already been eliminated. Of course, Christian Dalits are not treated by their community as though they are free from caste. It is an obvious inequality that harms Christian and Muslim untouchables. Many speculate that these exclusions have been upheld by fundamentalist Hindus who fear large numbers of conversions to Christianity, which has gained increased popularity in India in recent years.

To address this blatant injustice, a case was filed with the Indian Supreme Court in 2004, appealing for the rights of Dalit Christians and Muslims. Although the court ordered an investigation in 2005, the case had not been brought up before the court until April of 2007. Since that time, the case has been repeatedly postponed. The Court has displayed a distinct reluctance in responding to the plight of Dalit Christians and Muslims.

Untouchables are not the only outcasts in Indian society, however. The tribal peoples have experienced a similar exclusion. India's tribes account for a full 25% of the world's tribal population—67 million people.[4] They are considered even lower than the untouchables. Although some of these tribes live in cities, the majority are native peoples hidden away in the mountainous, rural regions of India. Tribal culture is very diverse, and whereas some tribal communities would appear indistinguishable from an Indian counterpart, other tribal villages seem to be remnants of a forgotten world. There are some tribal villages that still practice human sacrifice and cannibalism, although they are rare. Many Indians regard the tribal peoples as primitive and uncivilized. Most tribal groups live isolated from the rest of the world and have a culture all their own. Many of them are subsistence farmers, scratching a meager existence out of the mountainside. Because tribal peoples worship animist gods and goddesses, speak different dialects, and practice an ancient way of life, they do not blend in with the rest of India's society. In many ways, the tribal peoples are a society unto themselves, another India. Many tribes are true unreached people groups who have never heard of Christ.

Ironically, these people who have been shut out from India's culture have adopted parallels of their own. Shunned even more than untouchables, the tribal peoples have set up their own version of the caste system. It is a strange instinct in human nature that drives some people to imitate what has harmed them. In this case, the tribal peoples have a nearly identical caste structure of their own, tailored for their own society. Even in these small, scattered villages, the existence of caste prejudice and hate is real.

In the midst of these cultural difficulties, the reality of the Christian life offers a liberty that stands in striking relief to the problems of caste prejudice and violence. Paul's words to the Galatians have a powerful application for believers in India: "There is neither Jew nor Greek, there is neither slave nor free, there is neither male nor female; for you are all one in Christ Jesus" (Galatians 3:28, NKJV). As a bumper sticker pasted to the door of the girls' dormitory at Love-n-Care Ministries proclaims, "Freedom from Caste! Jesus Christ."

1

An Untouchable Childhood

A large crowd had gathered around the young man preaching on the street corner in Tuni, India. The blazing Indian sun was bearing down mercilessly on the whitewashed buildings and the dusty streets, but no one seemed to notice. Things were coming to a head between the dark-haired, dark-eyed stranger and the restless angry group in front of him. He had been to Tuni before, with the same message, and he had been warned. Despite their threats, he had come back, and his voice carried over the hubbub of creaking wagons, bleating goats, playing children, and merchants hawking their goods. He was determined to get through to these men and women. And he certainly had their attention. They had never heard an Indian talk about the gods the way he did. Although some in the crowd were listening with curiosity, a group of men standing in the front had heard enough. As the young preacher kept talking about Jesus, the tension in the air finally erupted into words of protest.

"We told you to stop preaching, Yesupadam!" one of the men shouted angrily. "We told you not to tell us again about this Jesus you worship. We have our own gods. You are following an American religion. We want nothing to do with your Western ideas. You have a foreigner's faith. Go away and stop filling our streets with the sound of your blasphemy."

As the man spoke, the crowd murmured its support. It was obvious that their collective anger and confidence was rising. White missionaries had come before, and had tried to tell them about Christianity. That had been one thing. But now this Indian man was calling them to turn away from everything they had known to follow someone named Jesus. He kept telling them that their gods could not hear them or help them—that their constant sacrifices couldn't erase their sins—that the one true God had conquered the punishment of sin by killing His son in their place. And that they could have God's love if they would turn to Him. The man's message was fascinating, but disturbing. He was trying to turn their way of life upside down.

But Yesupadam wasn't finished. "Wait! You don't understand," he protested. "This Jesus I am telling you about wasn't born in America, and Christianity is not a Western religion. Jesus Christ actually lived in the Middle East, in Asia. And the love that he tells us about is not just for Americans; it's for the world. He died to save Indians, too—he died for all of us."

But as he looked out over the faces before him, Yesupadam realized that his words had only increased their anger. He saw some of them stooping over and searching the dusty street for rocks, but he didn't pay attention. He kept on preaching, determined to share the good news with these people he had such a newfound love for—these people that hated him and his Christianity. He was amazed that the Holy Spirit had eliminated the hostility, anger, and violent retaliation that had dominated his life such a short while before. Instead of turning against these people who hated him, he now saw them as precious souls for whom Jesus had died. As he continued to preach from the Scriptures, the crowd began shouting at him and hurling the rocks they had been holding. At first he didn't understand what was going on, but he soon realized that they were actually stoning him. Even so, he refused to stop speaking. One large rock struck his right temple, and another broke his left hand, but he hardly noticed. As his head began to pulse and throb with pain, he instinctively reached up to touch the wound. He was surprised to see his hand come back wet with blood. Unexpected joy filled his heart at the sight, as he realized that the blood on his hands was for Jesus, the one who had shed all His blood for him. He had been counted worthy to share in the sufferings of Christ. He had once rejected Jesus, and now he was being rejected on the Savior's behalf. He had once shed the blood of his enemies in hatred, but now he experienced the honor of being reviled for his dearest friend.

And as Yesupadam stood before the seething crowd, he showed them the blood on his hands, saying, "See this blood? You did this to me, but I still love you. I still love you, because Jesus loves you."

* * *

But the story of God's work in and through Yesupadam Padipamula did not begin in Tuni. It began many years before in Srikakulam, the small village in southeastern India where he was born. Srikakulam in the 1950s was (and is today) worlds away from modern Western life. The road to Srikakulam was a rough red dirt road, winding through vast rice paddies that stretch to the distant hills beyond. The village itself was only a collection of a few streets and buildings, surrounded by modest huts and makeshift houses. Above the chaos of low houses, tiny storefronts stuffed with colorful wares, and lines of yesterday's laundry strung from tree to tree, stood two tall white Hindu temples—their ornate beauty a marked contrast to the humble village. The purity and opulence of the structures was striking. Most of the houses in the village were simple huts with thatched roofs extending nearly to the ground. Some of the wealthier families had homes with concrete walls, but these were few and far between. Like most other houses, Yesupadam's was little more than a large room—maybe 250 square feet— for the entire family of seven. The banana-leaf thatched roof was the only protection from the elements, and since there were no walls, the low-hanging roof doubled as a privacy screen. Walking through an entrance in the sparse stick fence meant to keep in the animals, a visitor to the Padipamula house would have had no door to knock on to announce his arrival. In fact, there was no entryway. Like most of the village homes, family and friends alike entered by bending over double to stoop below the low roof into the dark room within. With seven family members, the family's home had only the necessary items. A few beds made up on the dirt floor, a couple of pots and pans, a stack of blankets, a bag of rice (on a good week)—these were the household goods of an average Indian home. Not much more. Light came from under the roof, along with mosquitoes, chickens, and whatever else could find its way inside. Although many people in the village have electricity now, no one did in Yesupadam's childhood. His family lived "hand-to-mouth," owning very little, and doing backbreaking work for long hours in the rice paddies. His childhood, though shocking to a Western outsider, was all he had ever known. Since this was a normal lifestyle in his community, the hard labor and poverty hardly seemed unusual.

Yesupadam's parents were "untouchables," part of the lowest caste in India's rigid social structure. For Yesupadam and his family, "untouchable" was not a mere title to be discarded at will—it was a mark that defined their existence and their future. As the name suggests, people born into this caste were considered so degraded and unclean that those in higher castes would not even touch them. Untouchables lived in a different part of the village, walked on different roads, and went to different schools. They were identified and separated from the higher classes of society. Because untouchables were so despised, the Brahmin priests would not even minister to the untouchable Hindus who came to their small temple. So Yesupadam's father, P. Rajaratnam, stepped in to perform the sacrifices for the other untouchables in his community. He was a devoutly religious man, and although his life was full of hard labor, hunger, and poverty, he had not turned against the gods. He was very faithful to the monkey god in particular. Rajaratnam's existence as a manual laborer and Hindu priest was the only life he had ever known, and it would have been his son's inheritance if God had not intervened.

But one day, before Yesupadam was born, a Canadian Baptist missionary happened upon that out-of-the-way village and began sharing the good news of Jesus. A crowd of men and women from Srikakulam listened that day, and all of them walked away—all of them except Rajaratnam. He was inexplicably drawn to the missionary's message, to the story of Jesus' love and sacrifice. That day, Rajaratnam became a new man as he put his faith in Jesus Christ.

His decision was a personal one, but its consequences were anything but individual. It was no small commitment. For a Hindu to reject his religion and turn to Jesus Christ was a slap in the face of his family, his community, his ancestry, and his culture. It was a decision that almost invariably brought social rejection and even persecution. Because of these huge obstacles, it is unusual for an individual to turn to Christ if no one else in the village does. But Christ had become real to him, and Rajaratnam could never go back to his old existence. His community excommunicated him and his family disowned him, but he remained faithful. Although his wife, children, and neighbors remained Hindu, he began to live a radically different life. He abandoned his responsibilities in the Hindu temple, and refused to worship the gods he had once served. He quit smoking and turned away from the alcoholism that had gripped him in his old life. Instead, he devoted himself to prayer, often waking up at three or four in the morning to do so, praying so loudly that even the neighbors could hear. He was not an educated man, but he had some basic reading skills that allowed him to understand portions of his Bible. However, it was prayer that became the defining characteristic of his Christian life. Although he had no fellowship with other believers, and no encouragement from his community, Rajaratnam remained steadfast. Eventually, as a result of his example, several other men in the village became Christians. These other men saw the work that God had done in Rajaratnam's life, and the faithfulness of his love, and through this one man's example, they were drawn to Christ. Together they founded a small Baptist church.

Rajaratnam's youngest son was born after he became a Christian. Wanting to express his faith in God, Rajaratnam gave his son a name that he hoped would be prophetic: Yesupadam. The name means "the foot of Jesus," or literally, "Jesus' foot." It was Rajaratnam's prayer that one day God would use his son to take the Gospel to the nations.

It seemed unlikely that Yesupadam would fulfill his father's dreams. He was weaker than his brothers and sisters, and he suffered from anemia. It didn't help that the family's poverty often forced them to skip two or three meals a week. His father's job as a day laborer in the rice fields meant that when his employer didn't have cash for his workers at the end of the day, the family had no money to buy food for dinner. His mother did everything she could to protect her youngest son from the gnawing hunger and the deprivation of malnutrition. When he came home from school she would lay her hands on his stomach to find out how much he had eaten that day. Whenever she felt an empty stomach under her hands (which was usually the case), she would bring him some rice that she had saved to strengthen her small son. Yesupadam's extra ration of rice, however, was not enough to make him healthy and strong. He was small and painfully skinny, showing the early signs of malnutrition. Hunger had sapped his energy and muscular strength, so it took Yesupadam much longer than the other children to walk to school. Nevertheless, he was determined to go, as school was a haven for him. His mind was far stronger than his body and he quickly rose to the top of his class.

One day at the age of eleven or twelve, as Yesupadam slowly walked to school, he collapsed unconscious by the roadside. He had gone several days without food, and his body had simply shut down under the strain. Randall McNally, another Canadian Baptist missionary, had decided to take his family out in their Jeep on that same morning—down the very dirt road where Yesupadam had collapsed. Seeing the small figure crumpled and motionless on the side of the road, McNally thought that the boy might be dead. As he stooped to pick up the body, he realized that the child, though weak and malnourished, was actually alive. No other passersby had dared to defile themselves by picking up an untouchable boy, but through McNally's simple touch, this child who had been accustomed to rejection, distance, and scorn found that he was not "untouchable" to those who followed Jesus Christ.

Without wasting any time, McNally took Yesupadam to the hospital. The doctors discovered that his hemoglobin levels were dangerously low—only 15% of the normal level. It was amazing that he was even alive. Thanks to McNally's generosity and compassion for a boy that he had never even seen before, Yesupadam stayed in the hospital for two weeks, until he had recovered enough to return home to his family. Unfortunately, the underlying conditions that had brought on his anemia and malnutrition had not disappeared. His family was still poor and they still didn't have enough food to eat. As for McNally, he seemed to have vanished, and Yesupadam had no contact with him for several years.

Yesupadam's poor health was not the only thing that cast a shadow over his father's prophecy. Although he frequently shared the Christian faith with his son, telling him, "Jesus loves you. He died for you," Yesupadam did not really understand what those words meant. He had gone to the Hindu temple with his mother and to the Baptist church with his father and he was very confused about matters of religion. To make matters worse, tension began to build between Yesupadam and his father. As the boy grew older, he began to perceive his father as a strict, harsh man whose religion was limiting and demanding. Distanced by fear of his father's discipline and disapproval, Yesupadam had no desire to embrace Rajaratnam's Christianity. Although he was closer to his mother, her Hinduism did not appeal to him either. Growing up in a home with two religions, he chose neither.

This skepticism left Yesupadam without a religious perspective that could explain the world he lived in. He became increasingly aware of the intense poverty that surrounded him, and in high school he began to experience the discrimination directed against him and others in the untouchable caste. His elementary school was composed entirely of untouchables, but he was the only untouchable from his village to go on to high school. There he began to taste the bitterness of intense prejudice. The teachers would not let him sit with the other students, and they treated him differently than his classmates. As a child, Yesupadam had interacted mostly with other untouchables; as a result, the inequalities imposed by the caste system seemed remote and unimportant. But because the high school he attended was outside of his immediate community, Yesupadam began to witness the consequences of being an untouchable in a larger and more diverse setting. He noticed that there were certain roads designated specifically for untouchables, and that he was expected to get off certain other roads when a person of a higher caste came by. Sometimes the women bringing water from the Krishna (a sacred river nearby) would pour it out and start over if they met him on the pathway home, because they considered their water to be contaminated by the mere presence of an untouchable. If he begged for a cup of water, those who were kind enough to give him some would not even let his hands touch the cup. Instead, they would pour the water into his open hands, forcing him to lap it up as if he were a dog.

Most untouchables opted out of high school, their family's poverty driving them to manual labor and work in the rice paddies.

For an untouchable teenager, Yesupadam was fortunate to escape that fate. But school wasn't easy. The few untouchables who attended high school were made to sit in the back, and the higher-caste teachers treated them with contempt. One day the teacher decided to punish Yesupadam, and ordered him to stand outside. Left outside in the heat of the blazing sun for hours, Yesupadam was too weak and malnourished to withstand the strain and he collapsed unconscious. When his brother heard of it, he was so outraged at the teacher that he found him after school and hit him. But it wasn't just the teachers—even the other children rejected him. Once they discovered that he was an untouchable, they refused to become friends with him. He had escaped the rice paddies, but he could not escape the rejection.

Far from appreciating his opportunity to get an education, Yesupadam became bitter and hardened. Being classed as a Dalit (the name for the untouchable caste) seemed like a humiliating and inescapable curse. It was degrading to be subjected to daily reminders of his "inferiority." As he reconsidered his father's faith, he thought to himself, *If there is a God, why would He allow me to be born in an untouchable family, living in such rejection and shame? There cannot be a God—but even if there is, I could not love someone so uncaring and cruel.*

Yesupadam's resentment only grew as he realized the effect of Christianity on his further education. Although there were some legal and academic benefits reserved for untouchables by the government, Yesupadam was not eligible for them. His father had registered him as a Christian, and Christians were excluded from the government's help. He knew that he was a good student, and that he had the chance of getting somewhere with his life. But chained to his father's religion—one that he already despised—Yesupadam felt powerless to climb out of the poverty and ignorance of his family and community.

This volatile mix of experiences made Yesupadam a prime candidate for Koteswara Rao's teaching and mentoring. Koteswara Rao was a high caste man who had studied philosophy and humanism, and he had come to despise the injustices of his culture's caste system. As an atheist and a humanist, he turned to the writings of Karl Marx, and quickly became an ideological communist. Instead of living where he could make money and show off his abilities among other intellectuals, Koteswara Rao looked for a community in need of help and enlightenment. He was a larger man, robust and friendly, with an easy laugh and a love of good conversation. Koteswara Rao was looking for disciples, people into whom he could pour the convincing doctrines of equality and communism. He moved to Srikakulam when Yesupadam was 11 years old, and he immediately saw its untouchable community as a laboratory in which to implement his theories. His attitude toward caste and social position was revolutionary to those who lived in Srikakulam. He lived among the untouchables, even though higher-caste people had offered him a place to live. He started an after-school program to tutor the untouchable children, and he fought for the government to give them a better education. He studied homeopathic medicine so he could provide better medical care for those in the community, and he shared his possessions with those around him. He even wrote plays and dramas for the children to perform, setting up a sort of community theater program. Koteswara Rao was a true believer in communism, and it was evidenced in his everyday life.

The opportunities presented through his version of communism were very attractive to Yesupadam. For a young man who had been dismissed on the basis of his caste, the prospect of an ideology that dismissed the caste system seemed like a dream come true. Koteswara Rao took a special interest in the malnourished but remarkably bright young boy. As he began to tutor Yesupadam after school, Koteswara Rao began to tell him about communism. He promised that there was perfect equality in communism, that people could be brothers and sisters regardless of caste. He saw in Yesupadam the makings of a true disciple for communism—one with talent, drive, and promise. Yesupadam was saturated with bitterness and anger against the caste system, and Koteswara Rao fed those sentiments in his young pupil. He would tell Yesupadam, "The rich and those in the higher castes are drinking your blood and your sweat." Yesupadam was part of the after-school program, and so he spent every afternoon with his mentor. He learned Koteswara Rao's lessons carefully and well. He began to pose questions to this "communist missionary," and he found the picture that was painted for him in reply to be quite enticing. At the age of 11, although he knew little about what he was getting into, Yesupadam covenanted to be a life-long communist, signing his name in his own blood. At last he had found something he wanted to live for.

Yesupadam's father was angry when he realized that his son had fallen in love with such an atheistic and humanistic ideology, but it was too late for him to change his son's mind. Although he was unable to persuade Yesupadam to think differently, Rajaratnam continued to pray for his defiant son. Yesupadam had become convinced, even at that young age, that communism presented a better alternative than the traditional caste system he hated so much, and he had no room in his heart for the Christ his father had embraced so many years before. Communism implied atheism and since Koteswara Rao didn't believe in God, Yesupadam didn't want to either. He had wholeheartedly embraced the philosophies of his mentor as an escape from the confines of his family and his caste. He believed he had a future in communism, and he chose the allure of self-sufficiency and freedom over the drudgery of untouchable poverty and submission to his father's Christianity.

2

White Man's Religion

Toward the end of high school, the conflict between Yesupadam's dreams and the reality of his poverty intensified. He wanted to become a doctor and help the poor who, like him, were so often overlooked. He had seen how much a man like Koteswara Rao had been able to accomplish, and he was inspired by his example. He wanted to help others who had experienced the same prejudice he had endured.

But once again, Yesupadam found that two things stood in the way of his dreams: his poverty and his father's Christianity. Because of his academic abilities and untouchable caste, he qualified for certain college scholarships—scholarships that would enable him to go to college so that he could do something important with his life. But Christians were excluded from those awards. His teacher noticed this, and recommended that Yesupadam change his religion on the government forms so that he could qualify for scholarships. But when Yesupadam asked his father about rewriting the forms, his father's response was adamant and final.

"You would sacrifice your conscience and change your religion just to get money from the government? I will never allow it. If you can so quickly turn your back on your religion, how do I know that if you use that money to get some big career, you won't turn your back on me as well?"

Yesupadam hated his father for his stubborn refusal. He felt like he was being punished for his father's allegiance to a religion in which Yesupadam did not even believe. But no amount of angry words or emotional pleadings would change Rajaratnam's opinion—they only increased the bitterness and chilly distance between father and son. Yesupadam was convinced that his father had ruined his future and shattered all his hopes for success by insisting that his son tell the government he was a Christian—when in fact he was not.

In the midst of this conflict, Yesupadam's mother became ill. His siblings were all married and gone, so the responsibility of caring for her fell to him. He was already working as a day laborer and going to school, and now on top of this he was expected to do the cooking and the laundry for his parents—without the convenience of electricity. He knew his parents needed his care, but he hated every minute of it. He felt trapped and overworked, surrounded by responsibilities and obligations that seemed to keep him away from a bright future. Being his parents' caretaker only increased the hostility and resentment that he already felt. There seemed to be no way out.

The loss of the scholarship opportunity had deeply depressed Yesupadam, but he couldn't let go of his hopes for the future. He decided to apply for college anyway. He was ecstatic when he found out that he had been accepted to a good medical school. On telling his father the good news, Rajaratnam's curt reply crushed the dreams that his acceptance letter had encouraged.

"We have no money to send you to school, Yesupadam. I'm sorry, but you know that we can't pay to send you. And you can't go to school if you can't pay." For Rajaratnam, that was the end of the discussion. For Yesupadam, it seemed like a confirmation of his father's stubborn resistance to everything he longed for.

This new conflict, added to the mountain of old tensions, pushed their relationship to the breaking point—and Yesupadam to the edge of despair. On the day before the deadline for acceptance, their disagreement exploded into argument.

"If you don't help me go to school, you are cutting me off from every hope I have to live a good life, to get beyond all this," Yesupadam insisted.

"I am telling you, son, I just don't have the money," his father replied. "I have none to give you. I won't send you to medical school. Go into education instead—it takes less time and will cost you less."

As their voices and emotions escalated, Yesupadam felt overwhelmed by hopelessness. In anger, frustration, and despair, he rushed out of the house, telling his parents that he was going to go kill himself.

His angry words terrified his mother. From her bed, she cried after him, "Boy, come back here! Obey your father!"

But Yesupadam closed his ears to her and kept running until he got to the Krishna. He had every intention of throwing himself into the river, but for some reason he held himself back. As he stood on the riverbank, he realized that there was something stronger than his anger and despair—fear of death. What would happen to him after he died? He did not know, and that terrified him even more than the prospect of staying in Srikakulam for the rest of his life. Unable to throw himself in, and unwilling to go back, he sat in the darkness by the bank of the river for several hours, his anger and despair festering within him.

Within minutes, the entire village learned that Yesupadam had disappeared, and they began to search for him. Everyone fanned out to look for Yesupadam, but it was his father who found him as he was reluctantly returning home. Finding his son safe, Rajaratnam's panic, fear, and guilt were overwhelmed by relief. Rajaratnam ran to his son and embraced him eagerly.

"I had no idea you would act like such a fool over this," his father said. "If I had known how important it was to you, I would have somehow found a way to get the money for you."

The next morning, Yesupadam awoke to discover that the unbelievable had happened overnight. His father had miraculously come up with the 450 rupees he needed for that year's tuition. For his father, it was like coming up with a million dollars in the blink of an eye, and Yesupadam never knew how his father got the money, or what he had to do to get it. But however it had been obtained, it was now Yesupadam's, and he was finally able to realize one of his dreams—he was going to college. Yesupadam was overwhelmed with new hope and a sense of opportunity and freedom. His dreams for a better life had almost died, but by his father's sacrifice, everything had changed. Now he could escape the drudgery of manual labor, and the humiliation of poverty. Now he had a golden chance to make something of himself, to find something that would finally make him happy.

For a village boy like Yesupadam, college meant moving to the big city. For the first time in his life, he had a pair of sandals on his feet. For the first time, he was able to afford pants, instead of the cheap shorts he had worn all his life. He felt so wealthy with these new possessions. Now, finally, he could look like all the rich people who walked down the street wearing shoes and pants. He felt ready to take on the world.

City life was intoxicating to Yesupadam. Everywhere he looked, there were new sights, new sounds, and new experiences crying out to be enjoyed. Eager to explore everything he saw, Yesupadam began to lose sight of his long-term goals. In Srikakulam, he had dreamed of doing noble deeds and serving others. But when the opportunity came, Yesupadam fell in love with short-term pleasures instead. Without self-control, his studies began falling to the wayside. He began spending more and more time with his newfound friends. And when they started smoking and drinking, he joined them. He soon found himself lying to his parents in order to get the money he needed to support his addictive habits. Day by day—and rupee after rupee—Yesupadam was throwing away the opportunity for which his father had paid so dearly, but he was unwilling to admit this to himself or his parents. He was living a lie, deceiving not only his parents, but also himself. Every day, when his nagging guilt reminded him of his studies, he comforted himself by thinking, "I'll really focus on my studies tomorrow. Tomorrow I'll be more responsible." But tomorrow proved to be an elusive day, and Yesupadam couldn't break free from the bad habits he had so quickly formed. The freedom he had hoped for had spun out of control, becoming instead an addiction he could not escape.

Although Yesupadam had neglected his communist-driven medical dreams, he hadn't forsaken communism as a whole. Like many communist groups in India, the friends Yesupadam met in college used violence to further their ends. He joined the city's communist gang, and began devoting his time and energy to preaching their Marxist doctrines. As he imitated his new friends, he also began to embrace violence as a way to promote communism. In effect, he had become a communist missionary, and his message was simple: "Feed the poor; kill the rich." He and his friends taught the ideals of communism, and they punished anyone who disagreed with them. If the gang couldn't achieve equality through reason and dialogue, they were more than willing to try more physical means of persuasion. In fact, his gang took pleasure in beating those who exploited the poor. The violence didn't stop there—they even killed some who threatened them and their message. Communism may not have been a philosophy they wanted to die for, but it was one they were willing to kill for.

Yesupadam spent his days working for the gang, and his nights drinking with friends. There was little time for academic study, and it began to show. At the end of the year, Yesupadam found that he had failed every one of his courses. He dreaded returning to his family to reveal the results of his careless irresponsibility. *My poor family has given everything so that I could have this chance and now I have squandered it all,* he moaned to himself in shame. With a sinking heart, he headed for Srikakulam, his money gone, his hopes for an education dashed and his self-confidence shattered.

I feel like a guilty dog, slinking back to bear my punishment, Yesupadam thought as he entered the house. Unaware of his secret, his parents welcomed him, eager to hear about the successes of the boy for whom they had made so many sacrifices. Too afraid to tell them the truth, Yesupadam let them believe that he had studied all year and taken his final exams. But in India grades are published in the newspaper, and when his parents read the student rankings in the paper, they realized that Yesupadam had flunked out of school. They were devastated and ashamed, but too afraid to bring it up to their son. His suicidal declarations from the year before had put too much fear in their hearts, and they were unwilling to criticize him or do anything that might depress him further.

But even their silence condemned him. He knew what they felt about his failure, and what they thought of him. As he lay on his mat in his parents' tiny thatched house, he cursed his selfishness.

I won't do that to them again, he vowed. *I won't go back to school and bring more shame to them. I have to support myself for a change. I know I'm going to hate it. But no matter what, I'm not going to ask them for help again.*

His new reality was a slap in the face. Without the money to put himself through school, he had no choice but to work in the rice paddies. It was the same work that his ancestors had done before him, but that didn't make it any easier. It was grueling work. Yesupadam had to be in the field by seven o'clock in the morning to plant, weed, water, and harvest the vast rice paddies—all by hand. Hour by hour, he was bent double in the blistering sun, always working with plants by his feet. His hands, arms, feet, and legs were covered with sores from the fetid water that flooded the fields. His back, legs, and neck ached from the constant bending. He was miserable. And with every day of hard labor, Yesupadam carried the added burden of condemnation, knowing that he had brought this fate upon himself.

Just when Yesupadam had come to the end of his own resources and realized the helplessness of his situation, God provided him with a second chance. Randall McNally, the missionary who had picked him up from the roadside when he was a child, came back to Srikakulam and looked for him. He asked Yesupadam to come to Vuyyur and visit him. Somehow, he had heard that Yesupadam had returned to Srikakulam without a degree, and that he was reduced to day labor in the fields. Again, God had brought McNally in at a low point in Yesupadam's life; again, this missionary showed God's mercy to an untouchable so accustomed to rejection.

Yesupadam did not cut an imposing figure as he stood in the white man's office. His clothes were worn and shabby, hanging loosely from his thin shoulders; his skin was blackened by the merciless sun, and the skin on his arms and legs had broken out with sores from working long hours in flooded rice paddies. He was a sorry sight, and McNally pitied him. He offered Yesupadam the chance to go to school for free, if he would first train as a lab technician and then work at the Christian hospital afterwards for two years.

Yesupadam had not even dared to hope for a second chance like this. How could it be that a poor, malnourished, untouchable, living in an out-of-the way town could receive two opportunities to study at a university? Yet, there it was—an unsolicited offer for a free college education. Yesupadam accepted eagerly, determined not to squander his opportunity the second time around. This time he stayed focused on his studies. The Christian Medical Association of India where he studied was considered to be one of the best medical training institutions at the time, and at the end of the year, he had the second-highest grades in the Association. Yesupadam had committed himself wholeheartedly to his studies, and he reaped the benefits of his diligence.

He was offered a job at the hospital that trained him, but since McNally had financed his education, Yesupadam felt obligated to ask him if he was needed somewhere else. McNally asked him to come work with him in Pithaparum instead, and he did. It was a nice little town, not very large, but bigger than Srikakulam. Shaded by tall coconut trees and navigated by wide dirt roads, Pithaparum seemed restful and pleasant. Yesupadam began to find friends with similar interests, and he began to settle in. As he poured himself into his job as a lab technician, he realized that he genuinely enjoyed his work. He felt that he was helping people in need and fulfilling his communist ideals. Driven by these motivations, Yesupadam was willing to put in long hours of overtime—despite the fact that he was paid only 130 rupees a month instead of the 1000 a month that he would have received at a government hospital. He didn't mind because he felt that he had a job with real importance that allowed him to help others.

Working at a Christian hospital, however, meant that he was again thrown together with Christians—Christians who wanted to talk to him about their faith. But Yesupadam still had no interest in Christianity. Communism was his hope. He saw hypocrisy, politics, and power plays in the lives of those who professed faith, and he despised them for failing to live consistently with Christ's teachings. Jaded by the abuses of the Christianity he had seen, Yesupadam mocked the testimony of the sincere believers he worked with. This disdain, combined with a communistic defiance of hierarchy, brought some conflict between Yesupadam and his superiors. In a culture where "place" is religiously observed and authorities are endowed with the highest respect, Yesupadam's defiance was shocking. But he was neither Hindu (a religion that reveres hierarchy), nor Christian (which mirrors Christ's humility and service). He was a communist, and he served no man.

Two women in particular set out to share the Gospel with Yesupadam. His cold attitude could not hold back their compassion for the talented yet defiant young man. But Yesupadam shunned both their kindness and their message. Dr. Vining tried to tell him about Jesus, but he rebuffed her. Not to be pushed aside so easily, she asked her co-worker, Sandra Rickets, to help explain Christianity to Yesupadam. Sandra urge him to see the hand of God on his life.

"You've forgotten how poor you were, and how far you've come," she said.

But Yesupadam was offended and angered by those well-meant words. He felt that she was throwing his impoverished past in his face, and he began to threaten her.

"If you ever share about Jesus Christ with me again," he said, "I will see your end."

For years, it seemed, Christianity had surrounded him—first with his father, then McNally, and now his co-workers at the hospital. Yesupadam did not see the miraculous and merciful ways that God had used Christians in his life. Instead, he had convinced himself that it was a white man's religion, exploiting people rather than helping them. Yesupadam hated Jesus Christ's message, and he despised anyone who stood for Him. Besides, communism offered everything he needed to have a fulfilling and productive life... or so he thought.

3

More Than She Bargained For

Although Yesupadam's resistance to authority and contempt towards Christianity made him a difficult coworker at times, Dr. Vining and Ms. Sandra Rickets took a liking to him. He was a hard worker, and he was good at what he did. He stayed focused, he seemed reasonably moral, and he didn't flirt with the girls who worked with him. Even his communistic tendencies seemed to be waning—he was working too hard to devote much time to activism. Despite his faults, he was a good employee. However, Yesupadam's two-year contract was almost up and he was going to be transferred to a better-paying hospital. Dr. Vining wanted him to stay in Pithaparum, so she decided to play matchmaker.

Padmini was a diligent young woman who worked at the hospital, and she had become a special favorite of Dr. Vining's. She was very petite, her dark hair shining with coconut oil and coiled low on her head. She was quiet, but her hard work and quick smile caught Dr. Vining's attention—so much so that Dr. Vining shocked everyone by inviting the poor girl to come live with her in her bungalow. In a culture where boundaries of caste, race, and nationality were strictly observed, Dr. Vining's invitation was astounding. Dr. Vining decided to match up her two favorite employees, so she began encouraging Yesupadam first. Since arranged marriages were the norm, Yesupadam and Padmini were open to her suggestions. At Dr. Vining's encouragement, Yesupadam began to watch the slim young girl as she went about her work, and tried to learn more about her. He noticed that she was a hard worker, and though young, she was financially supporting her siblings' education. For her part, Padmini thought that Yesupadam was handsome, and she didn't seem to mind his communist leanings. They liked each other, so they decided to get married.

Yesupadam and Padmini had not consulted their parents to direct their marriage plans. When Yesupadam told his father about the intended match, Rajaratnam was not pleased with the arrangement. Padmini, being from a poor family, brought no dowry with her, and she wasn't from Yesupadam's hometown. Rajaratnam had wanted to arrange a marriage for Yesupadam himself, and had hoped that he might have made an advantageous match for his educated son. But Yesupadam was used to standing up to his father, and he was now determined to marry Padmini. So at last, despite the obstacles, Padmini and Yesupadam were married in February of 1973.

It did not take long, however, for Padmini to realize that she had married more than she had bargained for. Whatever dreams she had for her life as a married woman were dashed when Yesupadam left her to go drinking with his friends on their wedding night. This pattern continued night after night in their first years together. He would usually leave work and go drinking, gambling, and socializing with his friends until the early hours of the morning, and then stagger home, only to begin the same routine again the next day. Nevertheless, Padmini remained calm, patient, and loyal. The revelation of Yesupadam's true character brought out Padmini's as well. She never complained about his drinking, and she never threatened to leave. Instead, she would curl up outside the front door to sleep quietly until her husband returned from his night of carousal on the town. He would stumble over her passive form in the doorway, and they would silently go inside together for the night. The wall between them, though unspoken and invisible, grew by the day.

Yesupadam did not participate in his debauchery without guilt. He genuinely liked his wife, and he berated himself for treating her so badly. He knew that she was suffering because of his love for alcohol and gambling. When he came home and saw her quietly resting in the doorway, he would resolve to treat her better. But his remorse was no match for his bondage to his sin, and although he tried to change again and again, he found that he was unable to do so. Yesupadam, once again, found that the activities he once pursued for pleasure ruled his life.

This pattern continued throughout the first year of their marriage. One night, silent though she was, Padmini's despair reached a breaking point. Yesupadam was drunk as usual when he came home around 2:00 a.m., but he was sober enough to recognize that something was different. The familiar figure of his wife lying by the gate was strangely absent. Concerned, Yesupadam went to the front door, only to find it bolted shut against him. Drunk, confused, and agitated, he kicked the door in and found Padmini eating *ganneru*, a lethally poisonous fruit. Yesupadam realized immediately that she was trying to kill herself, and he rushed her to the hospital, where they pumped out her stomach. Padmini survived—and so did the baby she was carrying.

Yesupadam was shocked. His wife's suicide attempt had caught him completely off-guard. He knew that his lifestyle had affected her, but he had been deceived by her patience and perseverance. But even this brutal realization of her despair couldn't break his habits. Nor did the birth of his daughter, Suneetha. He spent all their combined income on alcohol, and Padmini had a difficult time saving enough to feed the family. And so for Padmini, the cycle of depression was unbroken. Yesupadam had saved her life only to crush her back against a wall of despair.

Not long after Suneetha's birth, as Yesupadam was making his way home after another long night of drinking, he noticed a strange thing. There were two women at the community well.

How strange, he thought. *Why on earth would two women be out at the well at this hour of night?* He decided to go investigate.

But as he drew nearer, he realized that there was only one woman—he had seen double because he was drunk. When he came closer still, he discovered that the woman at the well was Padmini. She was standing on the edge of the well, preparing to throw herself in. For the second time, Yesupadam had arrived just in time to prevent his wife from committing suicide. Ironically, the man who was driving Padmini to despair was the same man who kept on rescuing her. As he pulled her back from the well's edge, remorse overcame him. He clung to her, weeping and apologizing.

"I'm so sorry that I've treated you like this," he said. "I know what I'm doing to you is wrong." His sorrow was genuine, and Padmini knew it. Despite his behavior toward her, and in the midst of her depression, she still found herself liking this handsome, alcohol-addicted communist that she had married.

Padmini was pregnant at the time of her second attempted suicide as well. Several months later, she gave birth to a son, Sunil. She found her life quite busy with work and two small children, which made her troubles with Yesupadam a little more manageable. Yesupadam was occupied with work and drinking with friends. Although they lived in the same house, their lives became very distant from one another. That year, better job opportunities came up that would force Yesupadam and Padmini to work in different cities, but because of their emotional distance, physical separation seemed no sacrifice—especially for Padmini. Yesupadam's squandering of their money on gambling and drinking had made it difficult for Padmini to scrape together money for food, never even having enough to afford an occasional piece of fruit for the children. So in 1975,

Padmini moved with her mother and the children to Rajahmundry; Yesupadam went south to Visakhapatnam (Vizag for short).

In many ways, they were glad to be separated. Padmini had been doing most of the parenting anyway, and she felt no particular need for an intoxicated roommate. And Yesupadam now felt free to live the way he wanted. He found some like-minded communist sympathizers in Vizag, and they made good drinking buddies. Of course, Yesupadam would go up to Rajahmundry to see his family occasionally. Often he would come to visit the family so that he could borrow money from Padmini. His life in Vizag continued much as his life had been in Pithaparum—a headlong pursuit of the things that held his heart hostage. Yesupadam had no intention of changing his ways and no idea that God was about to take his life by storm.

4

God Breaks Through

It was a seemingly random relationship. Yesupadam needed a place to live in Visakhapatnam, and Prasanna Kumar was renting a room. Kumar had recently converted from Hinduism to Christianity. He noticed that Yesupadam had a Christian name, but it was also clear to him that his tenant was anything but a believer. Fresh with excitement about his own conversion, Kumar wanted others to have that same happiness. Kumar saw the hopelessness and dissipation in Yesupadam's life, and he longed to tell him about the love and mercy of God. He began praying and looking for opportunities to share his faith.

From his perspective, Yesupadam saw that Prasanna Kumar was a nice young man. Yesupadam admired his orderly life and his honesty, and he enjoyed Kumar's open friendliness. He knew that Kumar was a Christian, but he liked him in spite of that fact. It was a new kind of relationship for Yesupadam—he wasn't used to liking Christians that much. After all, Yesupadam had invested significant time and energy in disproving Christianity. He had told people that Christianity was a fake religion, designed by power-hungry men to exploit weaker people. He had even read portions of the Bible so that he could ridicule it. But he found Prasanna Kumar different than most other professing believers he had met.

In January of 1976, six months after Yesupadam moved to Vizag, Prasanna Kumar invited him to an evangelistic outreach geared toward young adults. Yesupadam saw Kumar's earnest excitement and desire for him to come to the meeting, and he didn't want to hurt Kumar's feelings. So instead of laughing him off, Yesupadam told Kumar that he would go. He didn't actually intend to go, but he figured that he could make up a good excuse and back out later.

In fact, Yesupadam already had other plans for the weekend. It was a holiday weekend and he was planning on going to the beach with some of his drinking buddies. When Saturday morning dawned, Yesupadam slipped out of the house early. He wanted to avoid any contact with Kumar—this way he could just say that he forgot about the meeting. But at around ten o'clock, as Yesupadam was standing in his friend's kitchen cooking up some chicken curry for their beach trip, he began unexpectedly to feel a heavy sense of guilt about lying to Kumar and leaving him in the lurch. He had ignored his conscience for so long that this new burden of guilt felt strangely heavy. Suddenly, Yesupadam decided that the only decent thing to do was to go back home and at least tell his friend that he wasn't going. He felt bad leaving a nice guy like Kumar in the lurch. It felt strange to go out of his way to be honest and straightforward, but he felt driven to it.

When he got home, he found Kumar neatly dressed and ready to go, pacing like a caged lion as he waited for Yesupadam. When he saw him, his face lit up.

"Great, you're here!" Kumar exclaimed. "Hurry up, let's go!"

Yesupadam meant to explain that he wasn't going to the crusade. But somehow, Kumar's joy at seeing him and the flurry of motion kept him from crushing his friend's excitement. He just couldn't say no and disappoint his friend. Suddenly, inexplicably, Yesupadam found himself in the last place he wanted to be—at a Christian outreach. He hadn't even had time to tell his other friends that he would no longer be going to the beach. Resigned to his fate, Yesupadam sat reluctantly at the back of the crowd and felt around in his pocket for his pack of cigarettes. He could only hope for a short meeting.

But as the main speaker was introduced, almost against his own will, Yesupadam became interested. The speaker had impressive credentials. Yesupadam had always assumed that Christians believed their religion because they were uneducated and stupid, yet this man had graduated with a master's degree from one of the best technological universities in India. He had received prestigious awards, and his wife was a doctor who had also studied at an excellent college.

This is so strange, Yesupadam thought to himself as the man began speaking. *These are educated people. Why on earth would they give themselves to a religion like Christianity?*

He had planned on cutting out in the middle of the meeting, but Yesupadam forgot about leaving as he listened to the evangelist. He was an engaging speaker, and the things he had to say were actually relevant. Yesupadam was curious and intrigued. He had never thought that Christianity could apply to real life, and yet this speaker talked as though Christ could actually change people. He didn't even go out to get lunch in between the messages. He just stayed in the campground, and moved closer to the stage. The afternoon session was not what he expected. The preacher brought up the subject of lust. He described it as a sin that started in the heart and the thoughts. He was applying Christianity to areas of life that made Yesupadam feel very uncomfortable. Did God care about his thoughts and his heart? As the speaker continued, he gave specific examples of what lust can look like. Yesupadam was astounded.

Those are examples from my life... how does he know what I did back in Pithaparum? That girl I got involved with, those thoughts I was thinking, that note I wrote and left for her...he's talking about me! Yesupadam *thought. No one saw me! And yet somehow, he is talking about every-thing I have done.* He was incredulous. For the first time, he began to see his sins as personal affronts against a holy God who saw and cared about his actions. Somehow, he knew that God had given the speaker a window into his soul. God was after Yesupadam's heart.

Suddenly, as he stared at the stage, Yesupadam saw another person above and behind the speaker. He couldn't believe his eyes—he had never seen a vision before, but there was no other explanation for the figure he saw in the sky. Yesupadam saw a man nailed to a cross. His hands, spread out, were dripping with blood. He recognized the man as Jesus Christ, the one he had rejected. Then, incredibly, the man on the cross addressed him in an audible voice. He spoke in Telugu, in Yesupadam's own language:

"Son, I have done all this for you. What will you do for me?"

Son. That one word crumbled in an instant the resistance and stubbornness built up through years of rebellion. For Yesupadam, an untouchable raised in bitterness and social isolation, being addressed as God's son revealed to him the intimate and personal love of Christ to a degree that took his breath away. Would the Christ of God take a violent, embittered Dalit and bring him into his family? This was a love he had never known, a love he didn't know existed. This Christ, whom he had always dismissed as a fraud, was now unquestionably real.

Weeping uncontrollably, Yesupadam immediately surrendered his life to the Lord without a single hesitation. A joy rushed through his being that he had never before experienced, and he realized that he was a radically different person than he had been only seconds before.

Yesupadam felt an outpouring of excitement like nothing he had ever known, and he left the meeting eager to do something about the knowledge that filled his heart. He had to tell someone. On his way home from the meeting, he suddenly stopped at one of the busy street corners and started shouting to everyone who was nearby.

"I have seen Jesus!" he shouted. "I have really seen Him! He is real, and He has changed my life forever!"

Yesupadam wasn't exaggerating the change he felt. His life had utterly transformed from that moment. He stopped drinking and hanging out with his old communist friends. Instead, he joined a group of believers in the Upper Room Fellowship, and they committed themselves to evangelism and prayer. Within that first week of coming to Christ, Yesupadam was baptized—both in water and in the Holy Spirit. An intimate knowledge of Jesus Christ had not only transformed his heart; it had changed every aspect of his life.

But Yesupadam's old communist friends did not share his excitement. Soon after his conversion, five of his former friends came to his house and abducted him.

"Enough of this Jesus business," one of his old friends said menacingly. "I can't believe you have gotten involved in such a pack of lies. You have to make a choice, Yesupadam. Either you come back to communism, or we are going to kill you. Don't be stupid."

Yesupadam's reply was confident and resolute. "I have experienced real life, life that I had never even imagined before I knew Jesus," he said calmly. "I could never go back to communism." And he began sharing about the new life he had in Christ. Of the five friends who had come to threaten him that night, two became Christians. The other three didn't dare to carry out their ultimatum.

Once Yesupadam had been reconciled with Christ, his next step was to restore his relationship with his wife. He wrote her a letter, pouring out his heart and describing to her how he had become born again. He apologized for the past, and told her how he had changed. Padmini received his letter and decided she had to investigate for herself. So she took the train to Vizag and visited her husband. The man she found was not the man she had married. To her amazement, Yesupadam was studying the Bible and preaching about Jesus instead of drinking and smoking. Padmini was floored. What was this Christianity that had transformed her drunken, deadbeat husband into a passionate evangelist who suddenly loved others more than himself? As Yesupadam shared the Gospel with her, the truth of his words and the testimony of his life overwhelmed her. She too gave her life to Christ.

Reconciliation to Christ and one another brought a freshness to their marriage. They wanted to reunite the family, but Padmini was unable to get a job transfer to Vizag. So they moved to Tuni together, and Yesupadam made a two-and-a-half-hour commute to Vizag every day. It was a long trip on the dirty, rusted old train. The cars were often overcrowded, filled with the smells of stale sweat and the sweet chai tea that the train boys constantly peddled from car to car. If he was lucky, he got a seat on a hard bench, close to the barred windows that let in the humid breeze and a view of the endless rice patties and lazy red-brown rivers. Often, though, the train was too full and Yesupadam stood in the middle of the crowded aisle. Uncomfortable though it was, his daily travels seemed like nothing compared to the reward of going home to his family. He and Padmini were like newlyweds for the first time, and the long commutes a small price to be paid.

Yesupadam found himself living in a fundamentally different world with a completely new set of priorities. He was no longer throwing his life on the altars of alcohol and communism. Instead, he was preaching on street corners, going to long prayer meetings with the Upper Room Fellowship, and integrating himself in a local Baptist church in Tuni.

Upper Room Prayer and Evangelistic Fellowship (URF) had started as a group of newly converted young men who were burdened with an intense desire to experience more of Christ through prayer and evangelism. They began meeting in the upper room of a Presbyterian church, and their prayer meetings soon turned into a gathering place for over one hundred young Christians who used Upper Room as a springboard for evangelism. They began spending their Friday nights in all-night prayer meetings, followed by evangelism all day Saturday. On Sundays they would go to their respective churches.

These men were also heavily involved in their local churches during the week, but in Upper Room they found other believers with a driving, urgent need to spread the news about the Jesus who had transformed their lives and given them such real hope. They felt that too many of the established churches had grown content and complacent. It was in URF that these believers found inspiration to share the good news of the Gospel. Together they pooled their meager resources and bought an old, dilapidated van so they could reach more villages with their message. Most of the men were married, but they were living as if they were single, giving all their free time to the work of the ministry.

Among such a group of zealous believers, Yesupadam stood out as especially committed and enthusiastic. He had an unusual passion for evangelism. He would often weep publicly as he shared the Gospel on the street corner, pleading with his listeners to reconcile with the living God. Yesupadam had a special burden for widows and the poor, and this was very evident in his behavior toward them. Not only would he entreat them to come to Jesus, he would show sympathy for their physical situations, comforting them and hugging them. The leaders began observing that Yesupadam was a man who would eat anything, sleep anywhere, and travel any distance, so long as he could preach the Gospel to those who had never heard it. He was truly and totally committed.

Although many of the leaders at Upper Room had great respect and admiration for Yesupadam, some others saw him as too passionate and headstrong—something of a firebrand and a rebel. His style of evangelism could be confrontational. Sometimes he would stand in front of the Hindu temples so he could get more attention. Often these temples were small thatched-roofed huts, while others were more elaborate concrete structures, ostentatiously coated with multicolored neon paint and guarded by large, wide-eyed idols that stared blankly into the distance. As he stood before the brightly painted figures and watched women offer their fragrant jasmine garlands to the gods, Yesupadam would begin cursing the Hindu idols and shouting, "Your god is a false god!" Some of the other men in the fellowship didn't approve of such offensive tactics.

Y. Jagga Rao, who was the president of URF at the time, re-members Yesupadam's early days well. Although Yesupadam was new to the group and a recent convert, Jagga Rao noticed his dedi-cation, consistency, and his love for the lost. He also noticed Yesu-padam's temper, which would occasionally get the better of him. Yesupadam didn't understand why others had less of a burden for those they preached to, and Jagga Rao even remembers Yesupadam taking some of the elder brothers to task for their lack of zeal. But while Yesupadam was upset by what he perceived to be lukewarm hearts for ministry, some of the elders were concerned for him and the repercussions of his evangelism on his family.

"Go home and spend time with your family, Yesupadam," Jagga Rao would say. "You need to be with them, not here. Go home to your wife. You need to rest and relax, and your family misses you."

"How can I go and rest with my family when there are so many around me who know nothing of Jesus?" Yesupadam would respond. "I have spent time with my family. Now it's time for me to devote myself to the lost." He adamantly refused to go home and relax.

Jagga Rao often became frustrated with Yesupadam's disobedi-ence, and he secretly wondered if Yesupadam were a celibate or perhaps an ascetic. What kind of married man lived as though he were single? It seemed astonishing.

The men in Upper Room Fellowship were seeing remarkable fruitfulness coming from their labor. Tens of thousands of people had come to Christ as a result of their faithful, tireless preaching in the towns and villages. Unfortunately, however, many of the established churches that these men worked from saw their zeal and determination as a threat to their traditions. The church that Yesupadam was part of in Tuni asked him to leave, and so he began to start prayer meetings in his home. Through his preaching, about 40 families believed the Gospel, and 40-50 people would regularly come to his home for prayer. These prayer meetings quickly turned into powerful events, as prophecies were given and people were filled with the Holy Spirit. Some of the young men expressed interest in going to the outlying villages with Yesupadam, so he began taking others out with him as he went to share the Gospel. It seemed that God was beginning a powerful ministry through Yesupadam—little did he know that God was soon going to send him away.

5

A Dry and Thirsty Land

One night, while he was asleep, Yesupadam had a strange dream. He was in a foreign land, in a place he had never been that was swirling with sand. It was a desert wilderness, but he soon realized that he was not alone. Men and women were frantically searching the landscape, looking for any kind of water to satisfy their consuming thirst. They looked panicked. Then he noticed the horsemen. They were armed with guns, hunting down the helpless people who were scattering through the desert. It was a frightening scene.

Strangely, the dream didn't fade in the morning. When he awoke, the intensity and reality of what he saw stayed with him. He was disturbed by it, and shared his dream with Padmini. He just couldn't seem to shake the memories from the night before.

As he began his morning devotions, he opened his Bible to Isaiah 21, and as he read, a strange and sudden clarity washed over him. Everything that he had seen in his dream was there in Isaiah. The whirlwinds in the sand, the sense of betrayal and fear, the horsemen, the oppressed people, and the desperate thirst for water was all described in great detail. Yesupadam read with amazement. The prophecy dealt with Arabia and Babylon, now modern-day Iraq.

Lord, you're trying to tell me something, Yesupadam prayed. *That strange dream, and now Isaiah? I don't think this is a coincidence. What are you trying to tell me?*

Yesupadam didn't get an answer, but he was still afraid. He didn't know what God was saying, but whatever it was seemed very disturbing indeed. Still wondering and anxious, he began to get ready for work, and took the long commute to the hospital in Vizag.

God, if you want me to do something, I need you to show me more clearly, he thought.

Soon after, a Christian co-worker approached him with some news.

"Yesupadam, did you know that there are job openings for lab technicians in Iraq?" she asked. "I thought you would like to know."

Yesupadam thought it was a strange question. He replied, "No, I didn't know anything about that. Why did you think it was important to tell me? But I'm not interested. My family is all here, and I'm happy where I am. Why would I want to go anywhere?"

"I don't know why I asked you that, actually," she said. "It was kind of an odd question, wasn't it? I'm not sure why I brought it up. I guess I just felt that maybe you're supposed to go. Why don't you just apply? It can't hurt anything."

It had just seemed like a strange conversation at the time, but when he shared it with Padmini that night, she immediately reminded him of the dream. God was answering his prayer with a clearer explanation, whether he liked it or not. It seemed clear to Yesupadam that God was directing his steps to Iraq. He didn't know why God would send him away, especially when it seemed like his ministry was gaining influence. He didn't really want to leave, especially when the dream had seemed so foreboding. But despite his confusion and reluctance, he knew that he needed to obey. So he sent a letter of inquiry to the Iraqi government in

Baghdad. He wrote it quickly, and sent it without a proper resume and information about his credentials. To Yesupadam's amazement, they responded immediately. Instead of sending him miles of bureaucratic red tape, the Iraqi government simply granted him permission to enter the country and offered him a job in a government hospital. Yesupadam saw this as a further confirmation that he was supposed to go to Iraq.

On hearing about the idea, however, the leaders of Upper Room Fellowship weren't as convinced. The salary increase seemed suspiciously large, and the leaders were concerned that Yesupadam was being lured in by the temptation of wealth. They were not as confident that God had spoken through a dream, and they couldn't see why God would send Yesupadam away. They strongly discouraged him from taking the job in Iraq.

Their stern rebuke surprised Yesupadam, after he had felt so much confirmation. He began to wonder if they were right. Maybe he was being tempted, or maybe his "signs" were just coincidence. So he changed his plans, and tried to forget about Iraq. It was hard for him to abandon this new dream, but he trusted his leaders. Besides, Padmini had now gotten a job in Vizag, so the family was together again. Things seemed to be working out. Still, for some reason, he didn't actively turn down the job offer from Baghdad.

Almost a year later, one week before Good Friday, Yesupadam and Padmini found themselves in an argument over some shopping they had done. It was just a little squabble over a botched shopping trip, but for some reason they both got very upset. Although they rarely argued, their disagreement escalated to the point where, frustrated and angry, they went to bed in separate rooms to pray and sleep. As he was praying, Yesupadam had another vision. In the sky he saw a hand writing in English letters, "I-R-A-Q." At the same instant, Padmini began crying loudly in the other room. Yesupadam rushed in to see what was wrong, and discovered that she too had heard from God that he should go to Iraq. Their irrational fight had driven them to pray. As a result, both had heard the same message from God.

Yesupadam decided that he could no longer stay in India. Again, he told the leaders of the Upper Room Fellowship of his plans to move to Iraq, and again they rejected his proposal as materialistic, disobedient, and rebellious. But this time, despite his respect for these men, Yesupadam decided not to follow their counsel. He knew that if he followed the advice of the elders, he would be disobeying God. It was a difficult decision, but Yesupadam knew that God was calling him to go. With Padmini's support, Yesupadam began to set plans in motion to move to Iraq.

He had to hurry. His visa was due to expire the next week, so he quickly booked a flight to Iraq and resigned from his job. His employers thought he was being impetuous, and they refused to accept his resignation. It was a stable, well-paying government job—something hard to come by in India. Why should he leave to go to an unknown job in Iraq? If it didn't work out he would return to India jobless in a tough economy. The hospital director turned down his resignation, and told him that he had to continue to work at the hospital.

"I'm sorry," Yesupadam said. "But I have to go now. My train to New Delhi leaves in a few hours. I told you I am quitting, and I can't stay any longer. My visa is about to expire. You'll just have to find someone else to take the position. I know you think this sounds insane, but I have to go to Iraq."

Only after much discussion, Yesupadam was able to persuade the director to accept his resignation. It not a moment too soon, for his train left the station only an hour later. Padmini, his only supporter, stood alone in the station to wish him farewell.

Things didn't go as smoothly as he had planned. When he arrived at the airport, he was confronted with a new set of obstacles.

"Where are the rest of your papers?" an airport official asked him.

"My visa is right here, and my ticket is right here. What else do I need?" Yesupadam asked.

"You need immigration papers to go to Iraq. If you don't have those papers, you'll have to go apply for them."

Yesupadam was desperate, and he began to beg. "Please," he said. "My visa is going to expire if I don't go tonight. There isn't another flight to Baghdad for a whole week. I can't wait that long. I've already quit my job to do this. Please let me go."

But it was in vain. He missed his flight, causing a chain reaction of delays. When Yesupadam went to renew his expired visa, the Iraqi embassy refused. Daily, he began the discouraging work of untangling the mass of red tape that engulfed him. He seemed to be getting nowhere. He spent 3 interminable months in New Delhi, dealing with immigration cards, visa extensions, health certificates, and other official documents. Stuck in a no-man's land between his home and his calling, Yesupadam began to feel very discouraged, and even questioned if he was right in thinking that this was God's will. In Vizag he had been so sure of God's clear call, but in the midst of so many obstacles, it was hard to feel so confident.

God, are you trying to tell me something? he asked dejectedly. *I thought I knew what you wanted, and even though everyone thought I was crazy, I've come here to follow your will. But nothing is working out. Did I hear right? Are you trying to tell me to go back home?*

He was ready to turn around and head back to Vizag. But when he wrote to Padmini from the capital, she responded immediately: "You are not coming home to Vizag. You are going to Iraq. This is God's will for you." Her unshakable confidence in God's calling strengthened Yesupadam's wavering faith. Encouraged, he determined to persevere through the mess of paperwork and delays.

He stayed with a friend's parents while he was in New Delhi, and he soon realized that God was at work even in what he saw as a setback. He had been focused on getting to Iraq, but God wanted to use him among the people in New Delhi, too. Yesupadam was the first man to ever walk into his friend's Hindu house with a Bible. His passionate testimony and daily life with Christ fascinated them. Through Yesupadam, the entire family became believers. He started a daily Bible study with them in their home, and soon found that he had a ministry to the Telugu-speaking Indians in New Delhi. With these evidences of God's activity, Yesupadam found that he had to fight against the temptation to stay. There was so much work to be done, and he was getting excited about the possibilities for ministry in northern India. Even though God was using him in New Delhi, however, he knew he was meant to be in Iraq.

After two failed attempts to board flights to Baghdad, Yesupadam was finally successful. In the airport, he met a very friendly Iraqi who offered to help him through his arrival to Baghdad if Yesupadam would assist him in New Delhi. Although he agreed to help his new acquaintance, he was suspicious. Why would this Muslim Iraqi go out of his way to help him? What motivated him? Yesupadam doubted that the man would make good on his promise, but to his surprise the man waited for an extra 2 hours while Yesupadam went through customs. Afterwards, he hired a taxi and took Yesupadam to his own home. When Yesupadam realized that a week-long religious festival had shut down the country and left him stranded in Baghdad, his new friend let him stay at his house without charge. Astonishingly, this new friend even gave him a month's wages to help him with his expenses, and told him how to navigate the oppressive government regime and get along with Saddam Hussein's authorities. Yesupadam had landed in Baghdad lacking enough money even for a hotel room. Without this man's help, he would have been stuck without resources during a week of holiday and he could easily have gotten into trouble with the authorities. This Iraqi whom Yesupadam had distrusted had turned out to be a Godsend.

Yesupadam needed all the assistance he could get in successfully navigating this new country. Saddam Hussein had come to power that very year, and the nation was in a state of flux. Government spies were everywhere, and it was dangerous to do anything to stand out from the crowd. Hussein's government was more secular than some of the previous regimes, so in some ways this made things easier for Yesupadam. He was assigned to Karbala—a deeply religious Shi'a city that, before Hussein's rule, had sometimes banned the presence of non-Muslims.

Yesupadam was installed in al-Husseini hospital, and began his work as a lab technician. He felt very deeply that his primary calling in Iraq, even more than working at the hospital, was to share the reality of Christ with those who had never heard of Him. He soon found this to be more complicated than he had anticipated. Few of his co-workers spoke English, and communication was quite difficult. He was anxious to share the Gospel, but was continually frustrated by the lack of opportunity. Yesupadam decided to learn Arabic, but it was slow going. He found Arabic to be a very difficult language—very different from the Telugu he knew. It was discouraging, having a burden for the lost and yet being unable to even talk to them.

After he had been in Karbala for about three months, he learned that it was a capital offense to convert any Muslim to Christianity. This obstacle, on top of his other setbacks, opened his heart to Satan's attacks. He began to question his move to Iraq all over again, and began to think that the Upper Room leaders had been right after all. The thought that he might be outside of God's favor drove Yesupadam to despair. Alone, without anyone to encourage him or support him, he even contemplated suicide. He began to think to himself, *If I'm not in the will of God, why should I even live?* But before he did anything drastic, he decided to write to a friend in Vizag. The reply he received changed his whole perspective.

"You are an ambassador for Christ," his friend wrote. "In some countries, ambassadors are busy. In others, they are not busy. But their title does not depend on their level of activity, but on the simple fact that the government has appointed them to that position. So it is with you. You are appointed by God, and even if you do not yet have much work, you are still called."

As Yesupadam read that letter, something broke within him, and he realized afresh that God had indeed called him to Iraq, even if the beginning had been difficult. Encouraged, he began to spend more time in prayer and Bible study. He sought out more spiritual food, and began listening to a midnight radio broadcast called *Back to the Bible*. He also received *Herald of His Coming*, a monthly magazine. Yesupadam had these resources and his own study, but no spiritual fellowship.

One day, the son of Yesupadam's landlord noticed his t-shirt, which said, "Jesus Christ offers peace and power." "That's true," Kamal said, pointing to the shirt.

Yesupadam was very surprised to hear such a calm affirmation of Christianity from his Muslim friend. "How do you know?" he questioned.

Yesupadam learned that the young Iraqi man had spent some time in Great Britain. Kamal had met a Christian man there, and after observing the depth of his friend's life, he had recognized the power of Jesus.

Seeing a wonderful opportunity to share the Gospel, Yesupadam began to tell Kamal his testimony, even though he knew it was illegal. After hearing Yesupadam's story, Kamal wanted to repent and receive Christ into his own life. Yesupadam was ecstatic—after months of waiting, God had dropped a perfect opportunity right into his lap! He gave Kamal his little green Gideon New Testament so that he could read and grow. But when Kamal's parents heard what had happened, they were not displeased. They began to put pressure on Kamal, even threatening him, until Kamal returned the New Testament. But Yesupadam continued to tell him about Jesus each time they were together, and slowly, Kamal began to grow in his faith.

Soon afterwards, Yesupadam began to have more opportunities to testify of the power of Christ. He began to share with an Egyptian doctor, as well as with a lab worker from the Philippines.

Yesupadam was then transferred to a remote desert village where he was lodged in a house with five other "married bachelors"—two Iraqis, two Egyptians, and one Filipino. Every evening, he would go out to the terrace and pray aloud for the other men he lived with by name. As he was on the terrace one night, Dr. Mazin, the hospital director and a devout Muslim, heard him praying and approached him.

"What are you doing?" he asked.

"I was praying," Yesupadam replied simply.

"Who are you praying to?" Dr. Mazin pressed.

"I was praying to Jesus," Yesupadam answered.

"But I heard you say my name," Mazin said, obviously puzzled. "Why did you do that?"

"I was praying for you, because Jesus taught his followers to pray for others," Yesupadam replied.

Dr. Mazin was surprised. "In our religion, we pray also," he said. "But I pray only for myself, never for anyone else."

Yesupadam began to share his testimony with his Muslim housemate. But while Dr. Mazin was amazed to hear that God had spoken to Yesupadam in an audible voice, he did not convert to Christianity.

Some time later, Dr. Mazin became sick with a cough. Instead of recovering, his condition worsened to the point where he could not even get out of bed without help. Yesupadam began helping him, knowing that this was an opportunity to display the power of Christian love. One morning, Yesupadam was helping Dr. Mazin to the table to eat the omelet he had prepared. The Lord prompted Yesupadam to pray for his friend, but he did not want to. *What if I pray for him and nothing happens? What if he reports me to the authorities?* he thought anxiously. *Who am I to make such a risky move?* He fought against the leading of the Holy Spirit, but he finally gave up the struggle.

Turning to his sick friend, Yesupadam looked him directly in the eyes and said, "Dr. Mazin, you have been sick for some time, and you have not gotten well. Can I pray for you? Jesus can heal you."

Dr. Mazin folded his hands, and responded, "Please pray for me." And he began to weep.

Yesupadam went to his room and got his Bible. He returned and began reading to Mazin from James chapter 5, telling him about praying for healing and anointing with oil. He explained that the power was in Jesus, not in the oil. As Yesupadam reached out to lay his hands on Dr. Mazin, he realized that he was shaking with nervousness. What if nothing happened?

The very instant that Yesupadam placed his hands on Mazin's head, the man cried out and jumped up from his bed.

"The moment you touched me, I felt a shock like electricity," he shouted. "I am healed!" Excitedly he began to call all the other men in the house up to his room so he could tell them what had happened.

Startled and scared by his response, Yesupadam tried to quiet Mazin. "Please calm yourself," he pleaded. "Don't you know that you are putting my life in danger by shouting this to the rooftops?"

Although Mazin's quieted his voice, the change in his heart was unmistakable and unshakable. His experience with Yesupadam, his healing, and the Gospel message changed his heart, and he became a believer. After Mazin's conversion, several opportunities arose for Yesupadam to share his testimony with other doctors. As they saw the story of his conversion confirmed and manifested in his life, many of them became Christians as well.

It was a day of rejoicing when Yesupadam went into the middle of the Iraqi desert to baptize the new converts in Razaza Lake. Only months before he had been despairing in Karbala because it seemed impossible even to share the Gospel, and now he was baptizing new believers. There they were, in a desert nation—both physically and spiritually. Yet even in the midst of this barren land, God was at work, and lives were being transformed. As Yesupadam stood in the hot desert, up to his waist in water, the parallel struck him. Christ had been at work even in the bleak Iraqi landscape, and now believers were being baptized into His name in this isolated pool of water. What a celebration it was! Although he had given up on his vision for God's purposes earlier, God had not forsaken him or those He was calling in Iraq. The words Yesupadam had read in Isaiah 21 came back to his mind with joy: "You... who camp in the thickets of Arabia, bring water for the thirsty... bring food for the fugitives" (Is. 21:13-14, TNIV). Just as God had instructed, Yesupadam had come to Iraq and brought a dying people true living water. It had seemed like a crazy idea. But in His faithfulness, the Lord had made a way where there was no way.

Those whom Yesupadam had led to Christ began introducing him to their friends, and his opportunities for sharing the Gospel increased exponentially. His ministry in Iraq began to bear much fruit. Because of the number of conversions, Yesupadam was able to plant three underground churches in Iraq—all of them filled with believers whom Yesupadam had personally led to Christ. The first church was planted in Karbala three months after the conversions began. A few months later, a second church was planted in Hyndia, and then a third in Hilla (near ancient Babylon). These underground churches were relatively small—twenty to twenty-five people each. Soon after, two other Indian Christians began to help Yesupadam in ministering to the Iraqi churches. They were amazed and encouraged by the eager response to Christ that they saw among a religious group that is traditionally very hardened to the Gospel. It is very difficult for Muslims to forsake Allah and the strict religious community of which they are a part. Following Christ and obeying His commands is treated as heresy and usually results in rejection and disowning by family, friends, and community. Often, believers experience strong pressure to return to Islam.

In fact, the process of a Muslim becoming a Christian is fraught with real danger. But God, as Yesupadam saw, was in the business of doing the impossible.

After Yesupadam had been in Iraq for three years, he began to have visions about visiting groups of believers in India. He began to realize that his work in Iraq was drawing to a close, and that God wanted him to return to his family and his people. This was confirmed by the Iraqi government, which began sending all foreigners away because of the Iran-Iraq war. Yesupadam had been safe the holy city of Karbala (the only city the Iranians wouldn't bomb), but God was sending him back to India. Six months after his visions began, confident that the Lord had work for him to do in Vizag, Yesupadam boarded a plane to go back home.

6

Preaching Alone

Yesupadam had left India for Iraq without knowing exactly what God would call him to, and he returned to India with the same unanswered questions. He knew that he would be ministering to Indians, but he did not yet know how, where, or to whom.

He soon found that his first ministry back in India would be to his own family. They had waited patiently for him during the three long years that he was in Iraq, but now Padmini needed him. Shortly after Yesupadam returned to India, Padmini discovered a lump in her breast. The doctor said that everything was normal, but Yesupadam felt uneasy and pressed for a biopsy. The lump was removed, and the results of the biopsy were normal. But the lump returned a year later, and this time, the verdict was far more serious. Padmini had advanced breast cancer—infiltrated carcinoma—and the cancer had already spread to the lymph nodes. The doctor told Yesupadam that his wife had only one to three months left to live. It was a devastating diagnosis.

Yesupadam decided that telling Padmini of her death sentence might psychologically weaken her resolve to fight the illness. That left him alone in the knowledge of her advanced cancer, and Yesupadam became very discouraged. He had felt called by God into full-time ministry, but now his wife was dying. How could he pursue God's calling without the love and support of his wife? And what about the children? Sunil and Suneetha were only ten and eleven.

One evening, as Yesupadam was sitting in the house and watching his children, Sunil and Suneetha began to play around their mother's bedside. They had no idea that their mother might soon be taken from them. The prospect of losing Padmini broke Yesupadam's heart. Overcome, he put his head in his hands, and began to weep. But in the midst of his tears, he had the distinct sense that someone had come alongside him. Then he heard an audible voice in his ear, saying, "Read Romans 8:28." Startled, Yesupadam got up and found his Bible. When he opened to Romans, he read; "All things work together for good to them that love God" (kjv). Even as he was reading the verse, God filled him with a new sense of faith and confidence. He felt compelled to express his trust in God, and he began to pray. "Lord," he said, "if it is Your will to take my wife, take her. She is Yours. But if You leave her here, we will both serve You."

Nothing whatsoever had changed in his circumstances, but the heaviness that had settled over Yesupadam's heart suddenly lifted. As always, he continued to pray for his wife, laying his hands on the lumps under her arm. But one day several weeks later, as he went to place his hand under her arm, he realized that he couldn't find the lumps.

Excited, Yesupadam called Padmini's doctor, but he said only, "I want to bring my wife in to see you."

"Why bother?" the doctor replied. "I already told you that I can't do anything for her."

But Yesupadam insisted, and made an appointment. When the doctor examined Padmini, he was stunned to find that she was completely cancer-free.

"What did you do with her?" the doctor asked Yesupadam, completely puzzled. "I can't imagine why the cancer just disappeared like that."

Yesupadam told the doctor of his prayers and the peace that the Lord had given him. The doctor listened with amazement, and could only reply, "Your God must be great."

They left the doctor's office elated, glorifying God for His gift of renewed life. Padmini was completely free of cancer for seven years, and she and Yesupadam committed themselves to serving the Lord in full-time ministry.

With his wife's cancer gone, Yesupadam turned back to focus on Upper Room Fellowship. Once the elders heard the story of God's remarkable work in Iraq—the new converts, the desire for revival in the midst of an oppressive regime, the three new churches—they realized that Yesupadam had been following God by leaving for the Middle East. They finally understood that he hadn't been motivated by the desire to make money. Eager to be reconciled with his old friends and mentors, Yesupadam resumed his old place at the Fellowship. But as he began to take in the circumstances at Upper Room, he saw that all was not well. The ministry which had previously been so focused on reaching the lost of India had unfortunately become sidetracked with internal power struggles. The infighting had weakened the leadership, and it became clear that the Fellowship needed a refocused vision and new unity. Yesupadam was surprised to discover that some of the leaders wanted him to take over as president. Although he was the youngest leader in Upper Room, his passion and desire for the mission was unmistakable. He was nominated as president, and the other elders hoped that his leadership might spark a revival.

God began to open new doors for Yesupadam during that time. One afternoon, a pastor from the primitive tribal area came to visit Yesupadam.

"Please come and preach at my church," he said. "I have heard of the ministry you have here in Vizag. I know that you are preaching God's news, and even going to other small towns. Please come to the tribal areas—don't overlook us. Do you know what it is like in the tribal villages? Those people have never heard of Jesus, and they are living in such poverty. They struggle just to live in those mountains. They are like animals, living without any hope, just trying to get through life. You must come help us."

Yesupadam had heard of the tribal people, but he had never really interacted with any of the tribes. He had never thought about how they lived, or that they had no access to the Gospel. The pastor's request opened up a whole new idea to Yesupadam—the idea of going to the unreached tribes of India with the good news.

The tribal peoples are indigenous groups that live hidden away up in the mountains. In the midst of a country that is working hard to modernize, the tribes seem like remnants of a lost time. Many of them live in small, mountainous villages just like their ancestors did, carving out a bare existence through subsistence farming and basic bartering. They are not considered to be true Indians, and the differences are noticeable even to an outside observer. With darker skin, broader noses, and stronger features, the tribal peoples look a little different than other Indians. Their women wear the same brightly-patterned clothing as other Indians, but they stand out with their love of large nose rings and earrings. They eat different food, worship animist gods rather than practicing Hinduism, and speak different dialects. Many "plains" Indians (so called because they are from the plains rather than the mountains) perceive the tribal Indians to be backward, dirty, and uncivilized. Indeed, much of territory in the tribal areas is extraordinarily primitive, as there are few resources available. Although some tribal peoples live in large villages that are equipped with electricity, running water, and maintained roads, most villages are nestled in the mountains, and make little contact with the outside world. Although there are tribal areas all over India, one of the largest reserves is in Andhra Pradesh.

Seeing their need for the Gospel, Yesupadam agreed to go preach at a tribal church. As he was driving his motorbike up the rocky mountain roads lined with forests and rice paddies, he saw a tribal man trudging down the path. His skin was baked brown by long exposure to the sun, and he was barely covered by a worn cloth wrapped around his waist and between his legs. His bony frame seemed barely able to support the heavy load of firewood he carried on his head. He had put in a full day's work gathering firewood and trekking around the mountain paths, but despite the hard labor he continued his slow journey through the mountains.

Suddenly but surely, Yesupadam heard the Holy Spirit nudge him: "Speak to that man about Me."

But Yesupadam did not want to stop and speak to the tribal man. He thought to himself, *We probably wouldn't be able to understand each other. His Telugu is most likely very different than mine. And besides, why should I take the time to stop now, when I am going to a church where I will speak to so many more?*

Yesupadam passed the tribal man, but the Spirit gave him no rest, and he finally turned around his motorbike and approached the man. He was amazed to discover that the tribal man could make sense out of his Telugu.

"Do you know Jesus?" Yesupadam asked.

The other man thought for a moment, and then replied, "No, I have never heard of that village before. But if you keep going to the next village, perhaps someone there will know where it is."

In that moment, shame flooded over Yesupadam. He felt unworthy to even call himself a Christian. Here he was, a man who knew Jesus, being fed daily by the Word and the body of Christ, experiencing life-giving fellowship with God. Yet he had been unwilling to stop and share his spiritual wealth with a man who had no idea that the Savior even existed.

Yesupadam told the man who Jesus was, and as he shared the Gospel, tears began to roll down the other man's cheeks. Sensing that he was ready to receive Christ, Yesupadam asked him, "Do you want this Jesus?"

But the man did not say yes—at first. His immediate response was a rebuke that cut Yesupadam to the heart: "I wish someone had told me earlier about Him. How can I refuse this good Jesus?"

Even isolated from any exposure to the Gospel, God had prepared this tribal man's heart to receive Christ. Yesupadam explained to him his need to repent of sin and put all his hope in Christ's dying work. He led his new friend in praying for forgiveness and asking for the gift of new life in Christ. Finally, they parted ways, continuing the way they began—the tribal man down the mountain with his load, and Yesupadam up the mountain to the church. Now, however, they were no longer strangers, but eternal brothers. Although Yesupadam rejoiced that God had worked in the other man's heart, he could not stop crying. He carried a new burden, realizing how many tribal people had never even heard the good news about Jesus. Yesupadam began praying as he went, asking God to give him opportunities to reach these tribal people who were so ignorant of Him.

From that day on, Yesupadam felt an unwavering burden to minister among the tribal people. But when he shared his vision with the other leaders at Upper Room Fellowship, they thought he was crazy. To them, it seemed clear that God was prospering the work in Vizag, and the other leaders wanted to stay where they were. They could not understand how Yesupadam could be willing to leave his comfortable position to minister to the tribal people. So Yesupadam went to the tribal areas alone, hiking through the hills, going to the remote tribal villages, sitting among the villagers, listening to them, and sharing his own life with them. Although he stayed on as the president of Upper Room Fellowship, it became a great personal struggle for him. He felt that there was an increasingly large gap between his own mission and the vision of the group with which he had once felt such unity. He began to pray about leaving. On their part, several of the leaders in Upper Room Fellowship began to compete for Yesupadam's position. Several of them felt disgruntled that Yesupadam should have such a primary role in the Fellowship when he was so young. He began to realize that the political maneuvers at Upper Room were detracting from its ministry. These power struggles and jealous competitions only increased Yesupadam's discomfort. After two years of deliberation, Yesupadam removed himself from his position at the Fellowship and sought a place where he could fulfill his call to the tribal peoples.

Yesupadam had left Upper Room Fellowship, but he knew it wouldn't be wise for him to strike out on his own. He needed a mentor—someone who could counsel, support, and encourage him as he ministered to the tribal peoples. He spent a year working with M.A. Paul, a friend in another local church who had a heart for tribal missions as well. It was a fruitful time for Yesupadam to learn about prayer and humility from a man who excelled in those areas. In 1987, Yesupadam and M.A. Paul went to a tribal convention in Madugula. Yesupadam preached on the third day of the conference, pleading with the tribal Christians there to reach their own people with the Gospel. He was becoming increasingly aware of the size of the work in the tribal areas, and he knew that he could not do it alone.

"Telling people about Jesus is not just for 'professionals,'" he said. "If you wait for pastors to come and share the Gospel with people who are in the villages around you, how long will you wait? There aren't enough pastors to reach all the millions of people who need to hear about Christ. Think about how many tribal people there are! Think of how it was for you, before you heard of Jesus—you had no idea of who Jesus was, or what He had done for you. Have mercy on your fellow tribes, and go to them with the Gospel. Please help us do the work. We must carry the good news of Christ's work to the tribal peoples together."

At the end of his message, he asked for the people to commit to bringing the Gospel to the tribal people. He hardly dared to hope that there would be others in the audience who would take his challenge seriously. But to his surprise, people came forward—not just two or three, but twenty-eight men and women pressed to the front, weeping and praying fervently with hearts broken for their own people.

Yesupadam realized that these people needed equipping if they were to be effective in impacting the tribal villages. Many were young believers with little knowledge of the Scriptures, and they needed to be taught the way of Christ more fully. They were passionate about reaching the lost for Christ, but they had only a basic understanding of Christ themselves. Together, Yesupadam and M.A. Paul committed to training these young believers in the Scriptures and the essentials of the Christian life. They decided to travel to Madugula one week out of every month. But when they made their first trip west to Madugula, to their surprise, none of the students came.

Yesupadam was confused. These twenty-eight men and women were so committed. Why had they not come? When he asked around, he discovered that the believers were not backing out of their commitment. Rather, their problems were economic. These men and women who had come forward and committed their lives to evangelism were day laborers in the rice fields, making barely enough to support themselves. It was impossible for them to come to classes without starving. As Yesupadam pondered this predicament, he realized that there was a need for a full-time school where young men and women could learn of Christ without concern for food and shelter. Without some level of financial security, even believers who longed to learn more about Christ would be unable to dedicate themselves to any degree of training. Somehow these believers needed financial help. That day, a dream began to form in Yesupadam's mind—a dream that would not be fulfilled for another two years.

In 1988, Yesupadam had a vision of two hands holding a globe. From all of the countries represented on it, six were impressed upon him: India, the United States, Canada, South Africa, Germany, and Sweden. Beneath the globe he saw the words, "Jesus Cares." As he studied the picture before him, he realized that it was a ministry logo, and that God was talking to him about starting a new ministry. He felt that God was directing him to plant churches and evangelize in India, and to help with discipleship among believers in the other five countries. Yesupadam awoke with excitement. God was giving him a plan, a sense of direction. It was a complete surprise to him—he hadn't been thinking about starting a new ministry or leaving M.A. Paul. That made it seem even clearer that God was the one directing him. As he prayed, he felt great peace about starting this ministry. M.A. Paul was reluctant to part ways with Yesupadam, but he gave his blessing as they parted on good terms.

Others, however, did not take his news graciously. When he shared his vision with other Christians in ministry, they just laughed at him. "Who do you think you are, Yesupadam?" they asked rebukingly. "What makes you think that you could go and offer anything internationally? You have no qualifications. How could you possibly afford to get overseas? Even if you could get there, why on earth would people listen to you, an untouchable from a tiny village in India?" They had a point. He certainly didn't seem like a prime candidate for international ministry. He had no connections to the outside world, only a halting grasp of English, and an upbringing that had better prepared him for manual labor than for international dealings. How could he ever expect to make a significant contribution on a global scale? Yet Yesupadam had learned over the years how to listen to the voice of the Holy Spirit, and he remained confident that this was God's calling for him. So as in other times, Yesupadam clung to God's direction for him, refusing to give up his faith in the things to which God had called him.

Even so, it seemed crazy. On January 22, 1990, Yesupadam and Padmini, together with five other people from the community, formed a committee to spearhead Love-n-Care Ministries (LNC). It was a humbling experience for Yesupadam to invite other church leaders and men in Christian ministry to come to his home and pray for Love-n-Care, especially when he knew that they didn't think his ministry had a chance. In their eyes, Yesupadam wasn't starting a ministry in response to a need—he was starting a ministry out of nothing. But the foolishness of God is wiser than the wisdom of men, and what looked ridiculous made perfect sense with the blessing of God.

Although he didn't know exactly why, Yesupadam decided to write up bylaws for the new ministry, even though the law didn't require it. Yesupadam had intended his ministry to be one focused on church planting and tribal evangelism, but the bylaws described the ministry's plan to minister to impoverished children, the disabled, and the sick. In reality, Yesupadam didn't fully intend the ministry to incorporate all of those aspects, and he found himself wondering why he was writing down these new goals. Little did he know that his bylaws were prophetic. Each purpose Yesupadam listed became completely accurate—in God's timing.

The first church meetings began in February with just Yesupadam, Padmini, and their two children. But the church began to grow. It was a small beginning—laughable by rational standards—just the seed of something only God could make grow.

Yesupadam had started Love-n-Care Ministries in Vizag, but his heart was with the tribes. Soon after the church was planted in the city, he began turning pastoral responsibilities over to the other elders in the church, and he devoted himself to the tribes. The ministry was so small at that point that there was no one to go preach with him. So he went alone. Hiking along forgotten roads and animal trails to get to the villages, he would arrive unannounced and begin to preach. It was easy to draw a crowd in the tiny hamlets that rarely had any visitors from the outside world. He experienced remarkable fruit. As he gave a Gospel call, explaining the reality of the one true God and the gift of His son to ransom sinners from destruction, many responded in new faith. The new believers would lead him to other villages where their relatives lived, urging him to preach there as well. Thus Yesupadam was led from village to village among the tribal people, sharing the good news of Jesus. Love-n-Care was a tiny, bare-boned ministry, but God was in the work, and it was growing.

7

Reaching the Tribes

In April of 2007, seventeen years after Yesupadam started Love-n-Care's work among the tribal peoples by himself, 219 pastors, staff members, and Bible students continued and expanded his work, hiking the mountain trails during the ministry's annual Tribal Camp. In ten days, they walked to 970 villages, sharing the Gospel and praying for miracles. Out of those villages, approximately 30 have been designated for church plants. Tribal Camp 2007 was momentous—now all the villages in the tribal district of Visakhapatnam have been reached with the Gospel.

It took years of hard labor, earnest prayer, and dedication to preaching God's word, and it was a watershed accomplishment. There are approximately 5,000 tribal villages—354,000 people—in Vizag's tribal belt. No one at LNC is aware of any other ministry in the state of Andhra Pradesh that has participated in evangelism and church planting on such a large scale in the tribal areas. Although at one time many had doubted that Love-n-Care Ministries would even survive, it has become abundantly clear that God is using this ministry to bear much fruit.

Indeed, the organization that once began on Yesupadam's front porch has now grown into a ministry that reaches many different people in a multitude of ways. Three children's homes collectively care for over three hundred children physically, academically, and spiritually. Three primary schools and a junior college provide education for those in the Bethany Children's Homes, as well as for students from the surrounding communities. LNC's ministry to the disabled trains polio victims (many of them amputees) in skilled work so that they can survive without begging in the streets. The hospital's highly respected medical staff provides quality health care to those who could not otherwise afford it. The Nursing School and Computer Training Center provide career training for the community. The printing press produces Christian books, tracts, and pamphlets in Telugu, Andhra Pradesh's primary language. The Discipleship Training Center teaches young Christians the basics of the Bible and practical evangelism, and prepares them for ministry (pastoral or otherwise). In 2005, LNC purchased the land to build a 100-bed hospital in order to serve more patients. Love-n-Care is also praying about the prospect of founding a Christian university. All of these projects and ministries display the love of Jesus, the Christian life, and the unity and faith of the church to a watching world.

But today, just as in 1990, Yesupadam's passion is church planting and evangelism in the tribal areas. The question of the tribal man that Yesupadam met on the road—"Why has no one told me of this good Jesus?"—still rings in his ears. Love-n-Care's ministry to the tribal peoples has grown out of a response to that plea for help.

In 1990, Yesupadam was the only one going to the tribal areas. It was hard work, and slow going. He would drive his scooter as far up the mountainsides as he could, but the roads quickly gave way to impassable trails, and he ended up doing a good part of the journeys by foot on the dry, red roads. He loved meeting new people day after day, sharing his precious message with village after village, each one unique and different. Sometimes he came upon small towns with bright whitewashed concrete buildings, a few straight streets, simple ditches for sewage, and gaudy temples painted in dayglo hues, carved idols staring blankly amid wreaths of jasmine and a mélange of other offerings. On other days, he would press deeper into the tall trees and thick undergrowth to a simple village of brown huts gathered around a cleared open space and a well. In those out of the way places, the only splashes of color came from the women's saris and the occasional piece of jewelry. Yesupadam was seeing many conversions and open hearts to the Gospel, but he needed help.

He remembered the men and women who had committed to serve the tribal peoples. They had so much passion, but no ability to leave their jobs and study God's word. Yesupadam searched for a way to support them so they could come and learn. A plan began to form, and Yesupadam found the doors opening for the first Discipleship Training Center. The ministry was less than a year old, but miraculously they found the means to support eleven men and one woman who came to study for a full year of biblical training. Some of these students were the same people who had committed themselves two years before. For a year, the students lived together in a small church building in Maredumilli—in the tribal area. Yesupadam and another pastor, Prem Sagar, provided the instruction. Prem Sagar lived with the students in Maredumilli, while Yesupadam traveled from Vizag to teach them. For these young people, used to hard day labor and the daily worries of finding food, the DTC was a whole new experience. With all their physical needs provided for, they were able to turn their attention to a new challenge—studying the Scriptures. They learned how to study their Bibles, how to understand what God was saying to them, and how to share what they were learning with others. It was a life-changing experience.

With the training of those first 12 students, Tribal Camp began to take shape. At first, it was simply a part of the training. Yesupadam and Prem Sagar would take groups of students out to tribal villages to preach the Gospel. Tribal outreach was at the core of the mission, and so it was only natural to equip the DTC students to do that work. Tribal Camp was less an innovative new idea than the logical fulfillment of a vital need. The DTC students were raised up for exactly that purpose.

By 1995, the school base had moved to Vizag, and the DTC had grown in size and expanded to include non-tribal students. At that time Yesupadam realized that a more concentrated effort would make better use of their resources. He thought about the eleven tribal *mandals*—large counties—surrounding Vizag. What if the Tribal Camp could expand and intensify so that an entire *mandal* could be reached each year? It would be a big project, but the idea excited Yesupadam. By gathering many pastors, ministry workers, and students into one effort, Love-n-Care could reach these many villages. Later in the year, he could send pastors to the key villages from the Tribal Camp and begin the work of church planting. It proved to be an effective plan. Since that time, the men and women who participate in Tribal Camp have labored faithfully to complete that vision.

Along with the other pastors and evangelists in Love-n-Care, Yesupadam is continuing his mission not only to reach every tribal community with the Gospel, but also to plant a church in every major tribal village. Since the state of Andhra Pradesh has one of the largest tribal areas on the Indian subcontinent, his dream is an ambitious one. The mountain regions of Andhra Pradesh hold tens of thousands of remote villages that have never heard the name of Jesus, much less met an actual Christian. Yet the passing years have not reduced Yesupadam's vision to a so-called "realistic" goal. On the contrary, Love-n-Care's vision for the tribal peoples has expanded to include tribal areas in the neighboring states of Orissa and Madhya Pradesh. Many thousands of people are starving for the Gospel, and few are going into those mountains to preach the good news—the need for action is desperately urgent. Rajaratnam had prayed that his son would become the foot of Jesus, but through Yesupadam's work, there are many who have become the beautiful feet of Jesus, carrying His good news with them wherever they go. Because of God's answer to that prayer, there are hundreds of men and women in Love-n-Care Ministries who are proclaiming that Gospel throughout India.

In the Western world, where churches are common, the ability to grow in faith with a community of other believers is a blessing often taken for granted. A church on almost every street corner is a reality so familiar to us that we fail to even notice it. It is easy for the well-fed to take food for granted. But the tribal people in Andhra Pradesh are starving with a spiritual hunger—an incapacitating starvation that has never been met. Desperate for something that will satisfy, these tribes have created their own gods, devoutly serving mute images that are helpless to answer their need. Filling these people with the eternal joy of knowing Jesus is the call of Yesupadam's heart. India has many poor, many disabled, many sick, many hungry, many orphaned, and many abused. Myriads of organizations (including Love-n-Care) are working to restore the broken. But those needs pale in comparison with the need for the Gospel. Through hearing the news of Jesus' atoning death and resurrection, tribal Indians are rescued from destruction. When churches are planted in those same areas, tribal Christians demonstrate and grow in the life of Christ together, and impact their communities with the daily testimony of the good news of Jesus.

* * *

Abraham and the village of Ootaguppa are just one example of the need and desire for Christianity in India's tribal areas. Like everyone else where he lived, Abraham had grown up worshipping the gods in nature—the supposed divine spirit within the trees, mountains, rivers, and sky. He had never heard of Jesus. His small, primitive village was completely isolated from the outside world, and he had never known anything different than the slow movement of days in a mountain farming community. But in the early 90s, Abraham went to a larger, neighboring village for a market day, bringing his produce to trade with people from the surrounding area. Above the colorful commotion of sellers hawking their wares and haggling over prices, Abraham heard the sound of a man preaching. In the middle of the bustling street, a man was talking about someone named Jesus. Abraham and a few other villages paused, curious to hear what the stranger had to say.

"I have traveled many miles to come and bring you a message," the man said. "It is a message that will change your life. You know yourselves that the gods you have served so faithfully are silent. You have done so much for them, but what have they done for you? Nothing. But I have come to tell you that there is only one true God."

As he listened, Abraham's heart resonated with the man's words. He realized that the preacher was right. The gods he had worshipped all his life were powerless. But how could this stranger prove that the God he served was really any different? He listened, curious.

"This God loves the people he made. So instead of making them pay for their sins forever, he sent his only son to become a man named Jesus. He died to accept the punishment we all deserve. He paid the price for our sins! This Jesus rose from the dead. But he does not live in a temple like the ones you see here in the village. If you trust in him and believe, he will come and live inside of you. This God who cared enough to die for you loves you and wants you to know him. Believe in this Jesus!"

Abraham was fascinated. And he was changed. As he listened, a desire was born to have God's life within him, and he gave his life to Christ immediately.

For a few precious hours, Abraham listened to the evangelist teach about the Christian life. He learned that God had written a book so that Christians could know God's will, and he learned that he could talk to God like a man talks to his friend. Since he had no Bible, Abraham clung to the miracle that he could know God in his heart through prayer. But the preacher had to leave, and Abraham finally had to return alone to his old world. It was the same village he had always known—the same people, the same family, the same way of life—but he was radically new.

Excited about all that he had heard, Abraham wasted no time in sharing the good news with the others who lived in Ootaguppa. After hearing Abraham relate the bare basics of the Gospel, about ten other villagers accepted Christ. He had no more instruction than those few hours of teaching in the marketplace, but he was the most learned Christian in the community, so Abraham began to pastor a church there. Miraculously, he was able to get a New Testament. He was barely literate, but his desire for reading God's word allowed him to learn from the Bible. Other than that, however, there was no contact with other believers or churches.

Christopher Tharapalli, the leader in charge of Love-n-Care's tribal ministry, stumbled across the village in 1993, during the annual Tribal Camp. As he talked with Abraham and the others, Christopher realized that these believers knew very little about the Christian life. They didn't even know drunkenness and alcoholism were displeasing to God. Christopher and the men with him began to teach them more fully about God's Word. The believers knew little of the Scriptures, but they were eager to receive instruction, and they quickly gave up their old habits. However, Christopher was only able to meet with Abraham sporadically in the following three years, teaching and helping as he could. Christopher was trying to help, but it was really the miraculous working of the Holy Spirit that guided this unusual church. By the time Love-n-Care was able to adopt the Ootaguppa church and provide more oversight for them, the church had grown to over 50 members, and Abraham and his brothers had planted two other churches nearby.

Both of Abraham's brothers were able to attend the tribal Discipleship Training Center for a year of Bible teaching and pastoral instruction. Although Abraham has never been able to attend the school, he comes down to LNC's headquarters in Visakhapatnam for conferences and teaching. Despite Abraham's minimal education, God has preserved the Ootaguppa church and given the believers there gifts of faithfulness, intercession, and love. The people are filled with a great zeal for God, and when Abraham asks them to come and pray, the church will often stay all night, laboring in intercession. They do not know as much as many other believers, but they are passionate about what they do know.

Abraham and the other believers in Ootaguppa needed a church. They needed Bibles. They needed to witness the lives of other Christians who were growing and striving to know Jesus. They needed teaching so that they could learn about the God they loved. There are so many other villages like Ootaguppa in the tribal areas. Without churches to model the joy of the Christian life, believers struggle and unbelievers remain unchanged. How great the need is, not only for evangelists, but also for *churches* to display the glory of Christ! The effect of a body of believers, living the truth together in the midst of daily circumstances, is an unshakable testimony. Abraham and the Ootaguppa church are a living example of God's provision in difficult circumstances, and they are a driving force in Yesupadam's passion for the tribal areas.

The need for tribal churches is great, but the challenges of accomplishing that task are also significant. The way of life among the mountain tribal people is very different from that of a "plains" Indian. Even though the two societies exist in the same nation, Indians going to the tribes are engaging in a cross-cultural mission. Christians going to the remote tribal areas must overcome the prejudice and disdain that they might normally feel for the tribes. In return, the tribal peoples must learn to accept and listen to someone with a different background. It is a challenge, but not an insurmountable one.

The tribal peoples generally live in smaller villages with greater poverty. Many of them try to provide for their families by chopping firewood, gathering mangoes, or growing crops. For many families, food is difficult to come by for three or four months out of the year.

Education is also hard to get, and the literacy rate in the tribal areas is only around seventeen per cent. In the remotest areas, polygamy is practiced, sanitation is unheard of, and clothing is not always worn. Alcoholism is a major problem, and extortion from outside traders is common. It is a difficult world.

Some tribal villages are just as developed as rural Indian villages. Both Indians and tribes labor under an oppressive caste system. In both cultures, women love bright clothing and intricate gold jewelry (though tribal women wear more facial jewelry). While the tribal peoples have broader features and darker skin than most plains Indians, they are ethnically similar. Both cultures eat similar kinds of food—although many Indians say tribal food is much spicier and cannot stomach the tribal *ambali* (fermented snails, rice, and water). Tribal peoples speak different dialects, but can usually be understood by Telugu speakers. Despite the differences, most plains Indian believers are better equipped to reach the tribal peoples.

Those who make the commitment to tribal outreach must also face the obstacles of geography and undeveloped terrain. With few roads (and even fewer passable ones), many villages are accessible only on foot. The tribal people, distanced by forests, mountains, poor roads, and cultural isolation, are rarely able to get to where the Gospel is being preached. For these people to experience the reality of the fullness of Christ, the church must be brought to them. Clearly, this is a demanding task, and it became clear to Yesupadam that he needed help. He needed someone who could bear the daily burdens and logistics of tribal ministry full-time. Christopher was that man.

Christopher had been a Christian for three years when he came to LNC's first Discipleship Training Center in 1990. Of average Indian build, Christopher is a handsome man whose startlingly bright smile flashes from underneath a well-kept moustache. The cheerful readiness and thoughtful maturity in his character are easy to detect even on casual acquaintance.

After graduation, he wondered what God wanted him to do with his life, and he began praying for the Lord to lead him. As he prayed, he saw a vision of barren lands cracking and crumbling from want of water. The desperation of the image stayed with him, but he didn't know what God was trying to tell him. God revealed its meaning to him at the Tribal Camp in Paderu in May of 1992. There he saw firsthand the needs of the tribal people, and the effect the Gospel was making in their lives. The vision returned to him, and he realized that the water in his dream represented the Word of God and the land thirsting for it was the tribal area. He felt that God was calling him to go and meet that need with the reality of Christ, the true water of life. He knew he must talk to Yesupadam about this calling, but it was an intimidating task. Indians are very deferential to those in authority, and are often uncomfortable with any actions that might overstep assigned roles. Yet Christopher knew that God was speaking, and so he approached Yesupadam with his burden to go to the tribal peoples. To his joy, Yesupadam said that he had been praying about that very thing. In fact, Yesupadam wanted Christopher to lead the tribal ministry. They both decided to pray about the idea further., to be certain of God's calling. After seeking God about the move for another month, Yesupadam decided to send Christopher out to the tribes.

So Christopher moved to the tribal area in 1993, along with John, another Love-n-Care pastor. They settled in Karakaputtu, a village of about 40 houses and 150 people. There were several new believers in Karakaputtu, so the pastors felt that it was a good base of operation. From Karakaputtu they were able to travel to the other seven villages in that *panchayathi* (district). After only six months, the two pastors began to construct a modest church building made of wicker and thatch. Not wanting to burden the impoverished tribal peoples, Love-n-Care supported Christopher and John. These two pastors were given 800 rupees a month—the equivalent of about $16 U.S. dollars—which they used for food, rent, and traveling expenses. Even though their rent was only 50 rupees a month, their stipend was not enough to cover their immediate needs. Sometimes they were forced to go without food. Even so, Christopher and John would often use their income to help support the sick and the poor. They would also buy little cookies to give to the children. In order to be generous to those around them, Christopher and John gave up food, and hunger was the price of their service. Yet, more concerned about the lost people to whom they were ministering than their own well being, these pastors found the sacrifice to be a joyful one.

In some ways, however, going hungry was the least of their concerns. Paul wrote that believers are "the aroma of death" to "those who are perishing" (2 Cor. 2:15-16, NKJV), and John and Christopher experienced that firsthand. After they had been in Karakaputtu for a year, ten leaders of the *panchayathi* came to visit. They wanted to talk to the pastors, but they were not looking to bestow any "Philanthropist of the Year" awards.

"We have decided that it is time for you to leave," one of the leaders said. "You have been telling our people about a new god. But we have plenty of gods—we are not interested in learning about yours. We don't need any new gods. You must go!"

After this brief speech, the leaders took their large walking sticks and began destroying the fragile wicker hut that was now the community's church building. The ten men and their sticks made short work of the building.

John and Christopher tried to plead with the vandals. "Please stop," they begged. "This is God's building. Don't destroy this." But the *panchayathi* leaders did not stop, and the pastors did not fight them.

"Now go," the leaders said. "Leave, and don't come back! If you stay, we will kill you."

"If you want to kill us, kill us," John and Christopher replied. "But we will not leave this place."

With those words ringing in their ears, the local leaders turned their backs on the ruin of sticks and straw and headed down the jungle paths to their own homes.

John and Christopher were frightened by the violence and the threats, but at the same time, they felt God's restraining hand upon them. They could not leave when God had told them to stay.

Around the same time, they experienced spiritual opposition from the local witch doctor. Christopher had a vision of the witch doctor sending an arrow into John's stomach. Trusting that the Lord was warning them, Christopher immediately found John and told him of his vision. They began to pray. Christopher's dream proved right—John soon began to feel a sharp pain in his stomach. They continued to pray, and after about fifteen minutes, the pain subsided.

The very next day, the witch doctor was brought to the pastors. He confessed that he had tried to harm them by using his witchcraft. The doctor had made special sacrifices to demons, asking them to attack John's stomach. But after John was healed, the demons returned to the witch doctor.

"Please pray for me," he said. "The attack that I sent to you has come to me. I feel poisoned all over my body, not just in my stomach. The pain has not gone away since it came yesterday. Please pray that your God would heal me."

John and Christopher agreed, and they prayed for the man who had persecuted them. He was healed, and the pain disappeared. But sadly, the witch doctor's heart was hardened to the compassion that Christ had demonstrated to him, and he did not repent and believe.

The villagers, however, were amazed. In their experience, the witch doctor's curses were usually fatal. They were impressed that John had been healed. They were terrified that the witch doctor had become sick from his own magic. The villagers were also astonished that John and Christopher were willing to pray for him, and even more so that their God had been willing to heal a defiant witch doctor.

In the same month, they experienced yet another threat. Much of the rural tribal area is a hideout for the militant communist guerillas, called the RSS. Because of their power (and sometimes their popularity), they have significant influence in the region. They had also informed John and Christopher that they were not welcome in the area. Despite all this opposition, and their own fear, they would not consider quitting the tribal ministry. Instead, they turned to prayer, sometimes staying up all night to pray for protection, to oppose witchcraft, and to ask for God's favor in the region.

After some time and much prayer, however, Yesupadam asked the pastors to move to Paderu. It was a much larger village, more central to the tribal area, and a better headquarters for the tribal ministry. But the change in location did not free them from the opposition they faced. The RSS were still hostile to them, especially when they traveled to other villages. Despite the resistance they encountered, John and Christopher (and now Joshua, a third pastor) continued to go far and wide with the good news.

One day, returning to a village where he had ministered, Christopher was stopped by several men from the RSS. They blocked the road, and wouldn't let him pass.

"We know why you've come here," they said. "But we are not going to let you come back to our village and preach about this Jesus again. Go back to Paderu." Their tone of voice was decidedly unfriendly.

"I can't," Christopher replied. "God has sent me to tell the people in your village about Jesus. I must go and preach about Jesus."

Immediately, one of the RSS men struck Christopher in the face. Years before, Christopher had devoted himself to the study of martial arts, and he had become very skilled in both defense and attack. Without thinking, he instinctively raised his hand to ward off the blow. But as he did so, he felt the Spirit's prompting: "Don't defend yourself." Instead of protecting himself or fighting his way through, Christopher knelt down in the middle of the dusty road, right in front of his enemies.

"Go ahead," he said. "Beat me."

The men needed no invitation, and they all began to attack Christopher with violent kicks and blows. But the village women were at the well, watching. When they saw the RSS men assaulting Christopher, they ran to his defense.

"Stop it! Stop beating this man!" they cried together, as they ran to protect Christopher. "Don't beat him! He is a god."

Although the RSS were violently opposed to Christopher and his message, the villagers had seen the power of God. When Christopher had come before, he had shared the Gospel with a woman who was dying of cancer. The cancer was in an advanced stage, and she had been vomiting blood. She had been to the hospital, but the doctors had discharged her, saying that the cancer had already gotten into her bloodstream and there was nothing they could do. She listened to Christopher, however, and he prayed with her every time he came to the village. Over a period of three weeks, Christopher's prayers were answered. The woman stopped vomiting blood, and her strength returned. Her friends and neighbors were astonished at this change in her, and they recognized that she was better because of Christopher's prayers. Knowing that such power could only come from heaven, these women assumed that Christopher was a god himself.

That healing, which saved the life of a cancer-filled woman, also saved Christopher through its testimony of God's power. Even though the Holy Spirit had prompted Christopher to offer his body to his assailants, the Lord was faithful to protect him through His own miraculous testimony. Instead of bringing the Gospel to the village in violence, Christopher's demonstration of love for his enemies enabled him to strengthen his witness to that place.

Again and again, Christopher and the other men who have shared Christ in the tribal areas have seen opposition. But every time an affliction has arisen, the grace of God has provided a refuge for them. Sometimes they are delivered, and sometimes they are given grace to endure. But always the Holy Spirit has filled them with boldness and power to continue their work until the mountains of India's tribal region resound with the joy of Jesus.

8

Flip Flops for Jesus

Sharing the good news of the Gospel with those who have never even heard the name of Jesus may sound exotic and glamorous. The reality involves hard work and significant sacrifice. Yet the joy of bringing the lost to Christ is a powerful motivator.

Love-n-Care's annual Tribal Camp offers a clear picture of both sacrifice and its reward. Every year, the students in LNC's Discipleship Training Center, ministry pastors, and other leaders target a specific region in the tribal area. Their goal is to blanket one tribal county with the Gospel of Jesus Christ. These evangelists walk from village to village, preaching faithfully until the entire *mandal* has been saturated with the good news. Between 1996 and 2007, Love-n-Care reached all eleven *mandals*, sharing the Gospel in each village and planting churches in strategic areas. And according to their broader vision, Love-n-Care is now going beyond Vizag's district to more distant *mandals* in Andhra Pradesh, Orissa, and Madhya Pradesh. However, Yesu-padam is not content to reach a tribal area once and consider the work finished. Teams also continue to go back to the previously reached villages. This "evangelism blitz" is the precursor to follow-up visits and church plants in the tribal area. Approximately two hundred and fifty churches have been planted in the tribal areas, reaching the church's village and those nearby with the Gospel.

Tribal Camp is a rigorous undertaking. For as long as it takes to reach the entire *mandal*—usually about two weeks or so—evangelism teams are sent out into the hills. Teams of eight men are assigned to a general region, and then split into teams of four to reach individual villages. Once a team reaches the village, the men go two by two as they share the Gospel. Women participate in the Tribal Camp as well, but stay near the base camp, because going into the mountains is both very strenuous and potentially dangerous. The women go to villages near the base camp along with key LNC leaders. Because they take the Campus Crusade *Jesus* film (and the projector, generator, and sound system that goes with it), the women travel to more accessible villages in a smaller radius from the camp.

The pastors and students who trek through the hills go for a week at a time, returning to the base camp on Saturday to share experiences, pray, and strategize about the next week. It is no exaggeration to estimate a weekly journey at 60 miles. Because this travel is done on foot, the men cannot carry enough food for the full week's journey. Rice is too heavy, and bread spoils after two days in such a humid climate. Rather, they choose to fill their packs with tracts and other materials to distribute in the villages. As a result, the evangelists are dependent on the hospitality of local villages by the middle of the week. The water in the mountains is unsafe to drink, but because the ministry does not have enough water filters for each team, most of the men go to the Camp knowing that malaria may be the price they pay for the souls they reach. Malaria pills could protect them, but they are too expensive. One pastor, Kiran, shared his perspective on this: "Many of us get sick after we go to Tribal Camp. We know that before we go. But for us, that is just the cost. It is still a joy to go." Kiran contracted a lethal case of cerebral malaria after Tribal Camp 2002. The doctors did not expect him to live, but God miraculously preserved his life.

The supplies they do have are not what Westerners would expect for such a long and strenuous journey. Although the roads are

usually poorly-cut, rock-strewn roads or small animal paths, most of
the men hike in $2 flip-flops. Without any backpacking equipment,
the men carry their supply of tracts and bread in simple knapsacks.
Without better backpacks, their loads become uncomfortable and
burdensome after a twelve-mile hike. Aside from physical discomfort,
these men also face the real dangers of wild animals—tigers, wild
boars, bears, and packs of wild dogs. Even the humans they meet
along the way can be dangerous. Bandits and guerilla forces have
made the mountains their home, and they are known for violence.
The circumstances for evangelism are obviously less than ideal, but
with peoples' salvation in the balance, the choice is obvious.

In one arena, however, Love-n-Care Ministries has seen great
favor. The radical communist groups that hide in the mountains,
known as the Naxalites, have not yet harmed any LNC pastors or
staff. The Naxalites are often highly educated people—professors,
lawyers, engineers, and others—who are angry and frustrated with
the caste system and the oppression of the poor. Frustrated with
the current political situation, the Naxalites have taken up arms
against the government and have found their safest hideouts in
the tribal areas. Although they have killed other Christian workers, including a pastor in December of 2003, they have recognized
that LNC is working to help the poor and needy. This is their goal
as well, and they see Love-n-Care as allies in the fight against oppression and poverty. Because they see the mercy and love of the
LNC people, they have not threatened or harmed the pastors who
preach the Gospel in the tribal areas.

The work is somewhat different for the women and pastors
who remain behind at the base camp. Usually numbering around
40 people, this group's primary responsibility is faithful interces-
sory prayer. They pray daily for protection, safety, good health,
food, and shelter for the men who are in the hills. But most of
all, they pray for God's saving grace to fall on those who hear the
Gospel, for radically changed lives, and for signs and wonders

to display the reality of His presence among the people. These women are faithful in prayer, crying tears of compassion for the lost, and pleading with earnest confidence for the salvation of those they may never see.

It is a considerable undertaking to transport the generator, projector, screen, and sound system for the *Jesus* film. However, the film has been very effective, especially in places where the language barrier is too great for communicating the Gospel. For people who have never left the mountains, or used running water or electricity, the very opportunity to see a movie is enough to stimulate the curiosity of young and old. Love-n-Care could greatly use a second set of equipment, which would enable them to reach twice as many villages with the film. But for now, the base camp team goes to one village at a time, sharing the *Jesus* film and the love of God to those who stop and listen.

The main thrust of the tribal camp, however, is centered in the teams of four that go farther into the mountains. For these men, their task is relatively simple and straightforward (but by no means easy). Although many villagers who live close to the major tribal communities of Paderu and Aruku have heard the Gospel, approximately 75% of those in the interior have never heard the name of Jesus. This means that the main responsibility of the missionaries is to explain who Jesus is, prove that He is real and that other "gods" are powerless, and tell how everyone can have a relationship with this loving, saving God. Before they enter a village, the team of four stops to pray and commit the village to the Lord, entreating Him to save the souls in that place. Once the men arrive at a village, they split into two teams and go to different parts of the village. They usually begin by singing songs, shouting, and clapping as they walk through the village, distributing tracts to every house. This usually draws a crowd and allows one of the men to preach. After sharing about the unique and essential claims of Jesus, the preacher offers his listeners a chance to respond and turn to Christ.

Yet more is often required. Most tribal people believe in many gods, and are reluctant to reject the religion of their ancestors for one all-powerful God... unless He proves Himself to be what He says He is. Because of the tribal people's need to see truth revealed, and because of the pastors' faith, the preachers always give an opportunity for people to come forward to be healed. They proclaim Jesus to be a living God, and one who is compassionate, gracious, and actively at work in the world. They declare that God can (and will) heal sicknesses, answer prayers, and cast out demons. Although many tribal people are initially reluctant to have others lay hands on them, God has continually revealed His power and love through personal prayer. Often, it is only after seeing miraculous answers to prayer that the tribal people will recognize and accept Jesus.

For most tribal people, having the favor of the head elder is almost as important as seeing that God is truly real. The chief elder in the village holds tremendous power over the rest of the community, and most people are reluctant to flagrantly reject his authority. If he takes a stand against Christianity, it is unlikely that many villagers will turn to Christ, even if they see miracles. On the other hand, if he welcomes the evangelists into the village or even converts to Christianity himself, the door opens for other villagers to follow.

Both of these elements were seen in one trip to the village of Kaniwada in 1991. This remote village in the East Godavari region is four or five hundred miles from Love-n-Care's headquarters in Visakhapatnam. Despite the distance, Christopher had heard of this village, and was burdened to tell the people about the sacrificial love of Jesus. Kaniwada was known to practice human sacrifice, and two years before, the villagers had murdered two traders who had gone there. The head man, who is in charge of the human sacrifice, was arrested but later released on bail. It was widely known to be a dangerous place, and as a rule, outsiders simply didn't go there. Even government officials were afraid of the village.

Christopher had a strong desire to go to the Kaniwada people, but others thought he was crazy. When a local pastor heard about Christopher's burden, he said, "Don't go up there. This is suicide. If you insist on going, expect to die." Undaunted, Christopher led a team of eleven other men up to the village.

After the passable roads gave way to footpaths, it was still a long way to Kaniwada. The men hiked 60 miles into the mountains. It took them about three days of steady travel. As they went, they preached in the other villages, sharing the good news with those they met along the way. Since it was the rainy season, and the clouds often emptied themselves on the mountain slopes, the men realized that a significant rain would soak their thin backpacks and ruin the tracts they carried. Not wanting to lose their precious cargo, they began to pray that God would keep their tracts dry. Five times over that three-day period, it rained all around the men, but not on them. Sometimes the rain was very close, only 100 feet away or so, but still they stayed dry. Seeing God's care for them and for the message they carried increased their joy and faith in the journey.

When they reached Kaniwada, however, they realized how intimidating their mission really was. The people did not appear to be friendly. They were taller and stronger than most Indian men, and their skin had a red tone rather than a brown tone. The Kaniwada men shaved most of their head bald, pulled the remaining chunk of hair back in a ponytail, and wrapped it in cloth. Their appearance seemed strange, primitive, and menacing. But Christopher and the others had gone too far to stop now.

They discovered that Kaniwada was actually seven villages instead of one. Providentially, they arrived at the village where the head elder lived. Christopher and the other men approached the head elder, explaining who they were and why they had come, and asking for his permission to preach. The head man had heard the Gospel while he was in prison, but had not believed.

His response to Christopher's request was simple. "Here," he said. "Heal my daughter. If your God is real, then heal my daughter, and we will accept this Jesus."

The elder's daughter was a woman about 25 years old, with a large tumor in her stomach. It was so large that she looked pregnant. She was so ill that she was in a stupor, unable to eat, and very weak.

Excited at this opportunity to soften the head elder's heart, the twelve men followed the elder to his house where his daughter lay. They surrounded her bed and prayed for her with anticipation and faith while her father and other villagers looked on from outside. They anointed her with oil and prayed over her for about fifteen minutes. Nothing happened. Undaunted, the men left and went to the guest house that the village prepared for them (a house normally reserved for visiting Naxalite radicals). Rejoicing that God was going to answer their prayers, the men gathered to pray for the woman for another hour before going to bed. It was early evening when they finished praying, and the team went outside to talk with the villagers.

"God is healing the elder's daughter," they told the people. "Have confidence that God is working in her!" The villagers watched these strange men curiously, but were skeptical of their claims. Were these men crazy? They had seen no change in the elder's daughter.

At daybreak, they heard a man calling for them outside their hut. It was the head elder. His daughter had been healed. The tumor had liquefied, and she was passing it through her waste. That morning, she awoke from her stupor and asked for food. It was a miracle, and no one could deny the power of God.

The men were at the largest Kaniwada village, with around 160 to 180 residents. Everyone had heard of the amazing healing, and an excited commotion began as curiosity about this new God stirred up. The men began preaching to an eager crowd, proclaiming Christ and inviting more people to come forward for healing. As a result, many more miracles happened—fevers were cooled, someone's knee was healed, and others were delivered from the tyranny of evil spirits. Out of the crowd of listeners that day, fifteen people trusted Christ. Christopher and the others encouraged them to go to Maredumilli on market days to speak with the pastor there and grow in their faith, which they did. Five months later, a church was started in the village of Boddalanka, near Kaniwada.

Using that first Kaniwada village as their base of operation, the team visited the other six Kaniwada villages over the next ten days. Even though they were preaching the Gospel in the villages, and some people had trusted Christ, they were still uneasy. The history of the place was too ominous to let down their guard, and they were very aware of their status as outsiders in Kaniwada. Christopher instructed them to stay close together and not to wander off. It was a dangerous situation no matter what, but there was some safety in numbers. One day, when the men went outside the village to relieve themselves, Peter lagged a little behind the group. When he realized how far ahead the others had gotten, he became very nervous. He hurried to catch up with his friends, but he was too late. Several strong men had been lying in wait for him, and he was ambushed. One caught his arms, while another tried to thrust a sleeping powder onto his face. Writhing and kicking, Peter somehow freed himself from their grasp and ran toward the others, shouting for help. Realizing that they would have to deal with twelve instead of one, the ambushers slipped back into the forest.

Still not knowing why the Kaniwada men had tried to capture Peter, Christopher and the others asked the local believers for insight. The Christians there informed them that the muggers were from the family responsible for the human sacrifice that year, and they were hoping to capture someone from the team. Every year, a family was selected to provide a human sacrifice for the villages of Kaniwada. The blood from that sacrifice was poured over a cloth, which was then divided up among the village families. Each family sprinkled the blood on their seeds, hoping that their sacrifice would convince the gods to give them a bountiful year of crops.

The responsible family had a year to provide a sacrifice, and if they were unable to find and capture someone for the sacrifice, they were required to offer someone from their own family. With so many outsiders living in their village for a time, the family had been hoping to use one of the team members for the year's killing.

While the situation at Kaniwada was unique—most tribal villages do not practice human sacrifice—the need for healing and dramatic evidence of God's reality is the same in every tribal village. Stephen, another pastor in Love-n-Care Ministries, experienced this during the Tribal Camp of 2001. A taller, dark-complexioned man with thick hair and a bushy moustache, Stephen has a serious expression and direct manner that reveal his intense personality. Stephen and his team of six (three men and three women) took a trip to a village about fifteen miles from the base camp. It was about a two-hour walk on animal paths, and they arrived in the heat of mid-afternoon. Three or four temples were scattered about, and gaudy, brightly painted idol statues were prominent fixtures in the village. There were about 250 people living there, and it was obvious that it was a religiously devout community; many had painted the marks of the gods on their faces. The men were dressed in loincloths, and the women wore no blouses under their saris. The children ran around the dusty paths, along with the village's pigs, cats, and dogs.

The team stood in front of one of the temples and began calling a crowd together. One of the women began telling the people about Jesus. Stephen got up and followed her, preaching about Jesus' proclamation:

> *The Spirit of the Lord is on me,*
> *because he has anointed me*
> *to proclaim good news to the poor.*
> *He has sent me to proclaim freedom for the prisoners*
> *and recovery of sight for the blind,*
> *to set the oppressed free,*

to proclaim the year of the Lord's favor.
(Luke 4:18-19, TNIV)

After explaining who Jesus is, and how He fulfilled that Scripture, Stephen invited the needy to come forward to be healed. One woman came up with her husband, a man about 50 years old. He was deaf, and because of severe cataracts in his eyes, he was blind as well. Stephen went over to him, placing his hands over the man's ears and his fingertips on the man's eyes, and he began to pray. He prayed for about ten minutes, but nothing happened.

Stopping to talk to the couple, Stephen explained what faith was. Although the man was blind and deaf, his wife was able to communicate with him. Stephen told the woman that "faith comes from hearing, and hearing by the word of Christ," (Romans 10:17, NASB). After she explained to her husband, Stephen asked him, "Do you believe that Jesus can make you well?" He did.

Laying hands on the man again, Stephen prayed again. After praying for about five minutes, Stephen felt that the Holy Spirit was saying that he had prayed enough. He decided to step out in faith and assume that God had healed the old man. Finishing his prayer, Stephen opened his eyes and said to the man, "Look at me."

Hearing his voice, the deaf man looked up at him and said, "I can see!"

Stephen was ecstatic. He had known that God could heal, and he had had faith for this blind-deaf man, but he had never before been used by God for healing. And now, standing before him was a blind man who could see, and a deaf man who could hear. He gestured excitedly to Nehemiah, one of the other pastors, calling him over to witness the miracle.

The tribal couple, on the other hand, were in shock—too surprised to even react. But the truth started to sink in, and when Stephen encouraged the man to testify before his neighbors, he took the megaphone and began telling everyone in the village what had happened to him. As he told of the miracle, the villagers looked at him in astonishment. Realizing that Jesus must be the true God, most of the village put their faith in Christ and trusted him for salvation. Rejoicing in the miracle, the villagers began singing and dancing. Stephen preached for another thirty minutes, telling the new believers how to pray and live a Christian life. Then he and the other team members committed the village to the Lord and left, giving praise and thanksgiving to God as they made their way down the mountain to the base camp.

Some stories are dramatic, like the healing at Kaniwada. Some villages produce immediate and impressive fruit, like one village where half of the people came to Christ after watching the *Jesus* film and seeing the power of God over demons. In some other villages, however, the work that God does takes a little more time. Although some testimonies are quieter and calmer, these "smaller" miracles are no less miraculous.

Such was the case for a village that two teams visited during the Tribal Camp of 1993. Both teams accidentally headed for the same village at one point, and began the long hike up the mountain together. It was getting late, but the men were tired, so they stopped to recover before reaching the village. As they sat resting and talking, they heard the roar of a tiger in the distance. Alarmed, they continued their journey with renewed speed and energy. The men were weary from their long days' journey, but as they slowed from fatigue, they again heard the roar of the tiger. Fearful of being caught, the men broke into a run, and made it to the village before dark. The threat of the tiger inspired great fear in them, but without that incentive, the teams would not have made it to the village before dark. And if tigers are a threat in the day, they are a greater threat at night. God had used a tiger's threat to hurry them on and protect them from the danger of wild predators.

When they arrived at the village, they found that about 300 people lived there, and that none were believers. One person, however, had heard the Gospel on a radio program. He had not become a Christian, but he had believed that Jesus was real. When the men from Love-n-Care came, they preached about Jesus' death and sacrifice for the sins of the world, and of His love for all who put their faith in him. Out of the crowd of listeners, there was only one convert—the man who had heard about Jesus from the radio station. It is unusual for one person to turn to Christ if no one else does, because the dangers of persecution and dishonor from friends, family, and community are great. But this man knew that Jesus was real, and worth the price he might pay. Even though no one else accepted the message of Christ's love, he was compelled to receive.

Out of 300, only one turned to Christ... but heaven rejoiced, and so did the men who preached. And that one man's testimony of conversion and revolution had a great effect on his village. He later went to Love-n-Care's Discipleship Training Center, and returned to his village to pastor a church. Because of his work there, God has brought 40 other people from the village to saving faith. The seed of faith has multiplied forty times over in that village, and God will only continue to increase his work in that remote village. Even when the outcome from evangelism seems small (or nonexistent), the men and women from LNC have faith, based on their previous experience, that God's work is persistent and effective.

9

Tribal Churches

Tribal Camp is an evangelistic adrenaline rush. Fast and intense, it is an amazing opportunity to reach thousands of people with the Gospel of Christ. Yet Tribal Camp alone is insufficient to fulfill the Great Commission. Jesus' followers are commanded to "make *disciples* of all nations" (Matt 28:19, NIV). Healthy, Bible-believing churches are needed in order to turn new converts into strong disciples. In many ways, Tribal Camp is just a preliminary step in the real work of planting churches and pastoring. The role of a pastor *begins* with evangelism, but it does not end there. For those who lead tribal churches with Love-n-Care Ministries, the life of a pastor is one filled with sacrifice, discipline, poverty, prayer, and most of all, joy.

After every week of Tribal Camp, the teams return from their journeys and compile information. By the end of the Camp, Yesupadam and the other key leaders are able to identify the most strategic villages for future church plants. Frederic (who leads the tribal ministry) and Krupa (who oversees the Discipleship Training Center) are heavily involved in this process, along with Yesupadam and several other pastors. These men must consider village size, relative location to other villages, the number of conversions there, and the commitment of the new believers, even as they rely on the Holy Spirit's direction. The number of villages targeted for church plants varies each year, and depends largely on the number of pastors Love-n-Care can afford to deploy into the field. In 2007, after 970 villages were reached with the message of the cross during the Tribal Camp, 30 were targeted for church plants later that year. To date, Love-n-Care has planted about 250 churches in the tribal area.

A month or two after Tribal Camp, John Frederic, Krupa, and the other pastors travel to the potential villages for church planting. They call this follow-up "second touch," and it is an important step in the process. Although they preach and teach, their main goal is to learn about the village community and confirm its potential for a new church. If they sense that the Holy Spirit intends them to plant a church there, the leaders will find a family to host the church in their home. Most of the villages that are originally identified for second touch agree to have churches planted.

Once a host family for the church is identified, the LNC leaders return with the men who will pastor the new church. It is too expensive to build a new home for the pastors and the church right away, so they must live with a family in the village. In most families in the tribal areas, four or five people live in one small room with a dirt floor and a thatched roof. Taking in two extra people is a great daily sacrifice of space and comfort for everyone. Usually, tribal pastors must wait for a few years to get married, because the tribal areas can be too dangerous. Yet even if a pastor feels secure enough to bring a wife to the mission field, poverty is a major factor. Few pastors can afford to raise a family in their first years of ministry. By choosing to pastor in the tribal area, many men decide to postpone having the companionship and support of a wife.

Eventually, the church grows large enough to erect a permanent building of its own. These structures vary widely in appearance. Some are little more than a roof on poles, providing shelter from the merciless sun. Larger churches might have low mud walls and even a tiled roof, with a bright sign or a painted message on the front of the building. Occasionally a church building is more elaborate, with cement walls, poured concrete floor, and a basic sound system with speakers that project loudly beyond the walls of the church.

However simple or involved the structure, the meetings look much the same. People come in softly, leaving their flip-flops (if they have shoes) in a jumble outside the door, and sit cross-legged on the floor. The men form neat rows on the right of the room, a homogenous group of neutral shirts and dark heads. In contrast, the women sit on the left in a profusion of color, with every imaginable hue and pattern blooming in cheerful chaos. The singing—sometimes accompanied by tambourines or congas—is loud and percussive, with rhythmic clapping and lively, repetitive melodies. Despite the hard ground and long messages, the church body sits still through the preaching of the Word, quiet and attentive. Often a pastor in a more rural area will preach at two or three churches in his area.

The work of a tribal pastor requires intense dedication, like the commitment of Arun Kumar. Arun Kumar is Yesupadam's nephew, and his body is deformed and partially debilitated from a childhood battle with polio. Polio is a common disease among Indian children, and it is responsible for many of the nation's crippled beggars. Polio victims often have several amputated limbs, and very few Indians can afford prosthetic replacements. Most are left to get by with whatever sticks or simple crutches they can find for support. In Arun Kumar's case, the disease struck the left side of his body. He walks with a severe limp, dragging the left side of his body with the strength of his right.

Arun Kumar became a Christian in 1990, at the age of fifteen. At that time he had a vision in which the Lord spoke to him three times, saying, "Arun Kumar! I have chosen you. I will lead you." Each time, he responded, "Yes, Lord. I will follow you." In the vision, he held a burning coal in his hand as a symbol of his commitment, and made a vow to follow the Lord for the rest of his days.

Soon after, he enrolled in Love-n-Care's DTC, and was sent as a pastor to Bakuru, a tribal village.

The other men were amazed at Arun Kumar's dedication. He only had half an able body, and yet he was determined to reach the mountain villages with the Gospel of Jesus. He limped along the rocky animal paths and the steep mountain slopes, visiting three or four villages a day. Most other pastors went in pairs, but Arun Kumar was alone in Bakuru. He assimilated himself into the tribal culture—eating their food, drinking their water, sleeping in their homes, using their language, and adopting their habits. When asked if he was lonely during that time, Arun Kumar replied, "Yes, I was lonely. But I was still happy, because I felt Jesus ministering to me when I was in the tribal area. And I knew that I was serving the cause of the Gospel, and that gave me joy."

Arun Kumar might still be in Bakuru, pastoring, praying, and ministering to the tribal people, had he not contracted a severe case of malaria. To protect his health, he returned to Visakhapatnam to live at the ministry headquarters. This disabled man who served God by facing wild animals on the mountain slopes of the tribal area now serves Him by running the Xerox machine and the international phone booth at the ministry's school. Although he longs to go back to the tribal area, he has contented himself with the humble work God has given him. He never complains.

So many of the Love-n-Care pastors show this same disposition: a complete willingness to do whatever the Lord calls them to, whether it be praying with faith for dramatic healings, sacrificing daily comforts, or serving others in obscurity. Newlyweds Kiran and Shalli showed such willingness when they began tribal ministry in Wantlamamidi. They had been married for only four days when they were sent to pastor in that village. Leaving friends, family, and home to live among a very different people in harsher conditions is a difficult thing, but even more so for a couple on their honeymoon—especially when they realized that they would have to share a 200-square-foot room with three other people for the first month! There were many challenges for the two honeymooners in Karakaputtu. But for Kiran and Shalli, the work of becoming a family for the spiritually homeless (and answering Yesupadam's call to minister to the needy) took priority over their own personal preferences. The people in Karakaputtu needed a pastor, so Kiran and his wife went immediately and without reservation.

In other situations, tribal pastors must sacrifice even necessary things. Because of the large number of pastors it supports in the tribal area, Love-n-Care can only provide their tribal pastors with a stipend of 800 rupees per month. However, it takes about 1500 rupees a month to maintain a subsistence lifestyle. The ministry's pastors do not usually take up offerings in their poverty-stricken areas, and as a result, they have to rely on God's provision and their neighbor's generosity for survival. Often, these pastors simply go hungry.

Christopher remembers many such instances when he worked in the tribal areas. February of 1995 was a particularly difficult time for him. Yesupadam had come to visit Christopher in Paderu, and brought a team of American pastors with him. Having nothing to set before his guests, Christopher approached Yesupadam in tears. He was heartbroken not to be able to bless his visitors with refreshments. It was only after pressing him further that Yesupadam learned the whole truth: Christopher had not eaten in four days. Yet to him, the hardest part was his inability to share generously with his well-fed American guests.

This frequent, gnawing hunger that so many pastors and their families have experienced is a constant reminder of their sacrifice. Yet their hunger has to be pushed aside for the pressing needs they must deal with daily. There is so much to be done, and regardless of their physical condition, these pastors are committed to the work of the Gospel. A typical day for a pair of tribal pastors begins at 5:00 a.m., when they rise to study the Word and pray. It is a time of peaceful communion with the Lord before the pressures and threats of daily life begin. Because this time with the Lord is so essential, it cannot be rushed or allowed to be a mere afterthought to the "real work." Often these men will spend about four hours in devotional time, fellowship, and planning for the day's events. By 9:00 or 9:30, the two pastors (who are always sent out in pairs) are usually on the road, setting off for a nearby village. They will typically try to visit four or five villages in a day, which is often equivalent to a 20-mile trip. They visit the same group of nearby villages repeatedly, strengthening the believers there and bringing the Scriptures to them. Fridays, however, are reserved for prayer and fasting. On Sundays, the pastors stay in a central village, and the believers from the surrounding area congregate together to participate in worship and prayer, and to hear preaching. Once a month, the pastors travel to Vizag to meet with Yesupadam, discuss the progress of tribal ministry, and pray together.

To many Western believers, it seems strange to take out so much time for prayer and fasting—time that could be spent ministering to people or organizing bigger and better programs. Even those who recognize the value of fasting and prayer often have difficulty spending so much time removed from the rush of daily life. But these Indian pastors realize acutely that they are helpless and ineffective without the presence of God. Extended times of quiet and solitude for prayer and fasting, therefore, are not their response to a sudden crisis or emergency. They arise instead from a practical awareness of *continual* need. Busyness and effort without Spirit-led direction and lives soaked in God's presence produce nothing of value. And so these pastors are unafraid to slow down their schedules and make time for prayer.

Their persistence in prayer is also necessary because of persecution against their work. Tribal Camp happens quickly, with little time for organized attacks against the Gospel. But when two pastors settle in a village and intertwine their lives with the communities that surround them, opposition often intensifies. Planting churches and daily evangelism bear greater long-term fruit than a "Christianity blitz," and they likewise produce more intense resistance.

Even when the enemies of hunger, poverty, and persecution are silenced, the life of a tribal pastor is a spiritual battlefield. There are many challenges inherent in caring for a people who are just beginning to experience the reality of God's Word and who are learning to fight personal and cultural sins for the first time. But those challenges produce rich and exhilarating fruit—lives irreversibly changed by the joy of knowing a true and loving God.

*Yesupadam (on scooter), as a young man,
with friend.*

Yesupadam's parents

Padmini

Yesupadam, Padmini, daughter, Suneetha, and son, Sunil

Hindu Temple

Temple site near village where Yesupadam grew up

Yesupadam with his mentor, Koteswara Rao

1983 | *Yesupadam baptizing Muslims and Hindus in Iraq*

Humble beginnings of LNC headquarters, Visakhapatnam, around 100 children

Tribal man

Tribal man at work in the rice paddies

Tribal woman

Tribal women

Storefront

Sugarcane Transport

Baptism of new tribal believers

Pastor Prasad with Sarah, the Dabbanda
woman raised from the dead

Tribal mountain area headquarters church and Bible School in Paderu

Yesupadam with Monika and Pastor Ingrid Bergner from Winnipeg who extended Yesupadam's first invitation to Canada

Naidu, the administrator of LNC's Vocational Disabled Program

2002 | *Police Commissioner distributing awards to disabled students from LNC's Vocational Training Center*

2005 | *Yesupadam with LNC pastors and leaders*

2006 | *Yesupadam leading an altar call at 'Revival India' Pastor's Conference*

LNC headquarters at Vizag, with Bethany Children's Home, DTC classroom, Bethany recoding studio, prayer hall, main office, and accomodations

Bethany Christian Hospital with nursing students

Bethany Christian Junior College building and students, Vizag

Bethany School of Nursing, Annual Capping and Candle Lighting Service

Bethany Discipleship Training Center 2006/2007 students, Vizag

Bethany Computer Center, School children learning

Church building at night

*Yesupadam and Monika in front
of his childhood home/hut with
village children*

Yesupadam speaking at a dedication ceremony

Pastor Frederick, Priscilla, and their children

Tribal Pastors

Tribal men gather at meeting

Tribal women gather at meeting

Appadu, a tribal man from Dabbanda who was raised from the dead, with his two sons

Yesupadam with family members

Yesupadam, Monika, and children,
Bethany and Benjamin

Yesupadam family (L to R): BACK ROW: *Samson (son-in-law, Suneetha's husband), Yesupadam, Monika, Daniel (Sunil and Kalpana's son), Sunil (son).* MIDDLE: *Benjamin, Suneetha (daughter), Bethany.* FRONT: *Samuel (Samson and Suneetha's son), Rose Salome (Yesupadam's mother-in-law), Shirley (Samson and Suneetha's daughter), Kalpana (daughter-in-law, Sunil's wife)*

Author Terri Whitaker with tribal children

Tribal pastors meeting with author's father, Dan Stolldorf

Author Terri Whitaker with town mayor and his wife

Prayer Mountain and site of planned 100 bed hospital, old age home, and mentally disabled home

Plans for Prayer Mountain project

10

Ask Anything In My Name

Love-n-Care's Tribal Camps often impact those who go to preach as well as those who are reached. For Prasad, the 1996 Tribal Camp profoundly shaped his perspectives on prayer, faith, and the power of God. In turn, his increase of faith had a profound impact on an entire village. A quiet man with a thick head of hair atop a set of thin shoulders, Prasad is a man who could go easily unnoticed—until he begins to speak. Then his reserved, almost shy demeanor contrasts sharply with the intensity and depth of his faith and reliance on the God for whom nothing is too difficult. Tribal Camp 1996 was the catalyst that propelled Prasad into a new understanding of trust and obedience.

During that month of outreach, Prasad saw God answer his prayers in new and miraculous ways and test his understanding of trust and obedience. Surrounded by other experienced and faith-filled believers, he was amazed by God's willingness to act. One afternoon, in the village of Marrigudem, he and his team encountered a woman plagued by demons. She had been telling the others in her village that she was going to stop the Christians from coming to preach. Not content with stopping the newcomers, she had been attacking and beating the believers living in the town. When Prasad arrived in Marrigudem, he found that the demon-possessed woman had attacked an older Christian woman, wrestled her to the floor, and was sitting on her. When the team walked in, however, she cowered in fear and tried to find a place to hide. The men began praying, and started to question her.

"Who are you in there?" they asked.

"I am a demon," she replied.

One of the men asked her, "Do you know who we are?"

"Yes," she answered. "I know that you are the people of Jesus. But I am going to cause so much trouble here that you won't be able to show your *Jesus* film."

Undaunted by her unearthly voice and confident words, Prasad and the other men boldly rebuked the evil spirit and ordered it to leave. Immediately, the demon left and the woman returned to her right mind. The team began praying, asking the Holy Spirit to overwhelm the village and take complete control there. As the Holy Spirit responded to this prayer, the believers began praying in the Spirit, sensing an outpouring of supernatural power and the nearness of God.

Unbelievers from the village had watched all of this happen, and they were amazed at the active reality of God's power. They kept telling the Christians, "Your god is great. Your god is great." Of the 500 who lived in the village, 200 committed their lives to Christ that day. One of the new converts was the very woman who had tried to stop the good news from coming to her village.

Prasad was almost as amazed as the unbelievers in the village. He was overwhelmed by God's power to bring even enemies to himself. Motivated by what he had seen, Prasad was filled with renewed faith and a new desire to see God at work. He began to fast and pray four days a week, interceding for the lost in his nation and asking for God to reveal Himself in power. As he prayed, Prasad was reminded of John 14:12: "He who believes in Me, the works that I do, he will do also; and greater works than these he will do" (NASB). Prasad began to meditate on Jesus' astounding words, and he took them literally. He began praying that God would use him to accomplish the works that Jesus did. As Prasad meditated on the implications of that verse, the story of Jesus raising Lazarus from the dead came vividly to his mind. What an amazing statement—that His disciples would do works like that, and even *greater* ones! Could it be true that followers of Christ could even be empowered to raise the dead in Jesus' name? Fueled by the stories of Scripture, Prasad continued to pray.

During that time, Prasad was focusing much of his ministry on a small group of believers in the village of Manyam Palem. While he was there, he heard that there was a village nearby that had never heard the Gospel. The caste system had gripped Dabbanda so strongly that it was actually divided into seven different mini-villages, each a separate caste. The villagers had completely estranged themselves from anyone outside of their caste, and the villages were poisoned with deep-seated prejudice and suspicion. When Prasad heard of this, he believed that he must be the one to go and share God's reconciling love with them.

There was no road from Manyam Palem to Dabbanda, so to get there, Prasad cut his own crude path through the underbrush with his machete to get there. Even after cutting a path, it took him four hours (after an already full day) to hike those fifteen miles. When he finally made it to the village, the sight that greeted him was anything but encouraging. The whole village seemed to have taken the day off to drown themselves in alcohol, and the drunken villagers didn't appear to be in any condition to hear about Jesus. They looked up at him strangely when he beat his way through the underbrush, as though they had never seen an outsider before.

"Who are you?" some of them asked. "What do you want?" They thought he had come to join in their celebrations, but Prasad declined their offers of alcohol.

"My name is Prasad," he said as they questioned him. "I have come here because I want to tell you about Jesus Christ, the Son of God." The people, however, were obviously not in a state to hear his message. Prasad stayed to pray for the village, and then returned home.

Although the first encounter had been discouraging to say the least, Prasad's burden for the lost in Dabbanda only increased. He began to fast and pray for the seven Dabbanda villages. After a week, Prasad felt God leading him to return. So that Sunday, instead of returning home after preaching at Manyam Palem, he set out on the long trek to Dabbanda.

When he emerged from the forest and underbrush, he made his way into the center of the village. Ignoring his discomfort at "making a scene," he lifted his voice and called the village to come and listen. As the men and women nearby turned their heads to listen, Prasad began to tell the people about Jesus. A curious crowd began to gather before him, stopping their evening tasks to listen to the stranger's curious message. But as he spoke, Prasad realized that the people were reacting strangely to his message. They were afraid. In fact, they were so frightened that they began begging him to leave.

"I don't understand," Prasad said. "What bothers you so much? Why are you so quick to reject what I'm saying? Jesus offers you peace and friendship with God—you don't have to be afraid."

Someone in the crowd spoke up. "If we believe in your Jesus, we will die." One after another, the villagers began to tell the story of their fear. They explained that, some time before, one man in their village had accepted Christ. But shortly after becoming a Christian, Polayya suddenly died. Superstition had reared its ugly head, and now they all thought that if they believed in Jesus, they would share Polayya's fate.

How could he shake their stubborn fear? Prasad didn't know what to do, so he simply prayed for them again, and went home. Yet even though he saw no way to relieve their fears and point them to the God of peace, he refused to stop going. Despite their apprehension and unyielding rejection, Prasad saw how much they needed a Savior. He also knew Christ's persevering compassion toward his enemies, and he was determined to show them the same love. Every Sunday without fail, he made the long journey to Dabbanda, praying for the people there and talking to anyone who would put up with him. But in three months, only one woman listened to his words. Lydia became a believer, but she was the only one who was willing to overcome her fear of death to experience God's forgiveness. Alone in her faith in a culture that insisted on social conformity, Lydia's decision to become a Christian was a very difficult one. Her conversion left her isolated and lonely, with only Prasad's weekly visits to strengthen her. No one else would believe what Prasad said about Jesus, and yet he still kept coming.

Late one morning, however, as Prasad approached the Golla Palem part of Dabbanda (where the shepherd's caste lived), he saw a noisy crowd gathered in front of one of the thatched huts. It was Appadu's house, and the people had gathered to mourn, weeping and wailing over his death. He had been ill all week, and had died that morning. Prasad approached the crowd, and as they told him what had happened, the story of Lazarus came to his mind again. With sudden clarity, Prasad knew that God wanted him to pray for Appadu to live again.

In the same moment, his own doubts assailed him. *What if nothing happened? What if he prayed and Appadu stayed dead?* Fear washed over Prasad as he considered the consequences. The whole village was crowded around the hut. *If I fail,* he thought, *I will be a laughingstock in front of everyone. My testimony to these people will be ruined; perhaps even my life will be at risk.* But as anxiety tried to push in, Prasad came to grips with the reality of the situation. *God was the one who told me to pray for this man,* he encouraged himself. *This is God's headache, not mine. If He tells me to pray, then I have to pray. He is in control of the results.*

So he obeyed. He went over to Appadu's wife and said, "Can I pray for your husband? I want to pray that God would bring him back to life."

Prasad's voice was quiet and unimpressive, but the impact of his statement hit the crowd like a thunderclap. Instantly, all eyes were turned on him and for a long moment, silence reigned. But as his words sank in, their ridicule began to surface. Like the story of Jesus with Jairus' daughter, the mourners began to laugh and scoff. "What are you praying for?" they asked Prasad mockingly. "He's already dead."

But Appadu's widow, realizing that Prasad could do no harm even if he could do no good, agreed to let him pray. After all, they had to wait for the rest of the relatives to arrive before the funeral anyway. This strange man certainly couldn't hurt a dead man by praying for him! So with her permission, Prasad approached Appadu's narrow wooden cot, which had been dragged outside with the body still on it. He knelt down on the red, dusty ground beside the bed, and placed his hands on the motionless corpse. Everyone crowded close to watch the crazy man do his work. Prasad forced himself to ignore them. And he began to pray.

Five minutes went by, then fifteen. An hour passed, and still Prasad prayed. Every few minutes, he would lift his head to see if anything had happened to the body. Nothing. And as Prasad watched Appadu, the rest of the village watched him. Still sure of God's direction, and undaunted by the disbelieving scoffers, Prasad continued to pray. Each minute seemed like an eternity, but he was unwilling to give up. God had told him to pray, and God had not told him to stop. For three long hours, from 12:30 p.m. to 3:30 p.m., Prasad prayed—180 minutes of ceaseless intercession for a cold, dead body.

Then he felt the corpse shake.

Prasad looked up. The arms and legs were quivering a little. His heart leaped with renewed faith that God was really going to do something, and he began praying even louder and harder. Then Appadu opened his eyes, and he was no longer dead.

Seeing this, Prasad immediately turned to him and said, "The Lord Jesus has given you back your life. Will you accept him as your Savior?" Appadu had not recovered his speech yet, but he nodded his head in agreement. He could hardly do less than follow a God who had just returned life to his body! Just minutes into receiving a new physical life, Appadu was born again into eternal life.

Then Prasad turned to the astonished crowd, who was by now clearly interested in hearing whatever he had to say. Minutes before, they thought he was completely insane. Now they had proof that the God he kept telling them about was real and compassionate. Taking the opportunity, Prasad began to preach. "See? Jesus has come to give you life. No one will die from believing in him. You think that if you become a Christian you will die, but I tell you that if you believe in Christ, you will wake up like this dead man."

Over one hundred villagers saw the dead Appadu become alive again. After seeing that miracle, 40 women trusted in Christ that day, as did Appadu.

Prasad returned home rejoicing, but he knew that there was more to be done in Dabbanda. He began to fast and pray yet again—this time for a week. "Lord, what will happen to this man?" he asked. As he prayed, he had a vision of Appadu coming toward him with his walking stick and a bottle of oil, falling at his feet. When he returned to Dabbanda a week later, Appadu was still bedridden, but he told the new believers of his vision. When he came back the following week, the vision was fulfilled, just as he had seen it—Appadu was well again, and coming to thank Prasad. The women were amazed to see that God had given Prasad a vision that came true.

That was the beginning of the Dabbanda church. At first, only the 40 women, Appadu's family, and the village children came. Besides Appadu, none of the men were willing to reject tradition and embrace Christianity. But Appadu's health after his resurrection was even better than it had been before, and the men started to take notice. Slowly, as they observed the power of God in Appadu's healthy body, their hearts were softened toward the Gospel, and the Hindu men began to talk to Prasad. That village began to believe in the power and love of God. But because of the strict caste system in Dabbanda, only villagers from Golla Palem (the shepherd's caste) came to church. It was the Golla Palem church, and the Golla Palem miracle—no one else from Dabbanda would have anything to do with it.

In 1998, a year after Appadu's rising, the brother of a Hindu priestess became ill with throat cancer. The people in Kapu Dabbanda were of the third highest caste, and although they had heard about Prasad and the miracle, no one would stoop to believe the religion of the lowly shepherd's caste. The priestesses' brother, however, was getting desperate. Although Appala Raju had gone to the hospital and taken treatments, nothing had helped. The flesh on his throat was rotting and blackened. He could speak normally, but he had to wrap a bandage around his throat to cover the decomposing flesh. Finally, despite his connections to the Hindu temple, Appala Raju went to the Christian pastor who seemed to know a living God. Prasad shared with Appala Raju about Jesus, and then he anointed his neck with oil and prayed for him to be healed. The next day, Appala Raju's wounds began to heal and dry up. After two weeks, he was able to remove his bandage and return to work. Several weeks later, his throat was completely healed and he was free from pain.

Appala Raju believed in God's power—indeed, his own body testified to it—but he was not willing to accept Jesus Christ as his Savior. The social cost was too high. His sister, a Hindu priestess, was also very opposed to his conversion, and he succumbed to her pressure. Nevertheless, his healing had a strong impact on the people from Kapu Dabbanda. The people from that part of the village were of a very high caste, and had not lowered themselves to attend church with the villagers from Golla Palem. But Appala Raju's healing fueled their interest. Because of this powerful miracle, the head elder in Kapu Dabbanda—Dhali Nayudu—became a follower of Jesus. Typically, the head elder in a village sets the tone for the entire community. Few people have the strength to accept a religion that the head elder rejects. Dhali Nayudu, then, played a vital role in the village's openness to Christianity. His conversion allowed the rest of the people to express their interest in Christianity. Prasad experienced a new level of favor from the people of Kapu Dabbanda, and some of them even began coming to church in Golla Palem. The presence of two castes in the same building was another miracle in itself. They would listen as Prasad preached, and some even had faith to ask God to heal them from some of their illnesses.

Seeing the impact that he was having in Dabbanda, Yesupadam asked Prasad to pastor the new church there. Under his care, the believers began to grow in their faith and influence in their community. But God was not done yet. One Sunday morning in 2001, as the congregation was singing, Prasad saw a woman periodically go outside and return a few minutes later. Sarah, a new Christian in her thirties, had been severely ill with malaria for about a month. She suffered from intense fevers and had been unable to eat. In spite of her weakened condition, Sarah was determined to go to church. She convinced her daughters to help her walk to the church building. Once she arrived, she sat in the back of the church on the cool concrete floor. Feeling very ill during the meeting, she went outside into the sunlight. Many tribal people believe that direct sunlight will help relieve a fever. Even though her fever returned during the meeting, Sarah refused to leave.

After the meeting, Prasad was talking to a visitor from Nepal who was working in the area. Suddenly, he heard a commotion in the back of the building, and when he went over, he saw that Sarah had collapsed on the floor. Her friends and family had crowded around her, trying to revive her, but could not.

In Dabbanda, Indians check for signs of life by pouring water into the body's open mouth to check for air bubbles or swallowing. They also believe that, if the person is alive, the water will be beneficial to them. But when they poured water into Sarah's mouth, it just ran out the sides. She was dead. Her three daughters began weeping and mourning, and as the other believers realized what was going on, they began to cry as well.

Prasad came over and checked for Sarah's pulse, but found none. As he saw Sarah's frail form lying on the concrete floor, he remembered the words of the Dabbanda villagers from years before: "If we believe in Jesus, we'll die." Several thoughts rushed through his mind. He was afraid that if a Christian died in the church, the unbelievers in Dabbanda would return to their old fears. At the same time, a jealousy for the glory of God came over Prasad, and he was unwilling for the Lord's name to be dishonored by a death in the church. His resolve was strengthened by Appadu's resurrection four years before, and by Jesus' promise in John 14:12: "Anyone who has faith in me will do what I have been doing" (NIV).

So once again, Prasad began to pray over a corpse. This time was different, however. Now, with a crowd of believers by his side, he did not pray alone. Although the others had a smaller faith, they were willing to pray with him.

After Sarah died, she felt a strange swirling, twisting, and turning sensation in her head and body. At first she was confused, unable to figure out what was happening. But as she focused on her surroundings, she realized that she was on a path in the woods, and that the path split into two just ahead of her. A large, intimidating man stood in the fork of the road, beckoning her to follow him down the darker path.

Frightened, Sarah immediately refused him, saying, "No, I won't follow you. I believe in Jesus. I will take the other way."

The dark figure, however, was insistent. "You must come with me," he said. "I was the one who brought you here." He tried to force her to come with him. Terrified, Sarah called for Prasad to come help her. Suddenly she saw him by her side.

"Why are you here?" she heard Prasad ask.

"I don't know," Sarah answered.

"Then come with me," he said, and he began to lead her down the path filled with light. Just as suddenly as he had emerged by her side, Prasad disappeared. Then Sarah opened her eyes, and saw her daughters, friends, and pastor crowding around her. She was alive again, and completely unaware of what had gone on since she collapsed. Prasad was happy to tell her the good news—she had been dead for about half an hour, but through the prayers of the saints, God had given her life back to her.

From the "living" side of things, Sarah's death and resurrection had looked quite different. Sarah had been dead for some time before Prasad came over. After realizing what was going on, Prasad and the other believers had prayed for Sarah for about ten minutes. Then he called her name repeatedly: "Sarah! Mother Sarah!" Then they had sat quietly for about five more minutes, and Sarah had opened her eyes.

Five minutes after she awoke from the dead, Sarah was able to get up and walk. Sarah was not "only" raised from the dead—she was completely healed from the malaria as well, and she never suffered a relapse. In fact, she walked home from the church that afternoon without any assistance.

Because of Sarah's testimony, the remaining unbelievers in her family put their hope in Christ, and the Christians who witnessed and heard of her resurrection were greatly emboldened in their faith. The visiting Nepalese man at the church that Sunday accepted the Lord and was baptized. And the entire village was again compelled to face the power of a living God who calls Himself both the Resurrection and the Life.

Dramatic changes have taken place in Dabbanda through Prasad's ministry there. Even so, unity among the various castes seemed slow in coming. But in 2000, Dabbanda's church building was erected in the *center* of the seven caste-villages. The Christians there have reconciled their class differences, and now they even eat together. This sort of acceptance, regardless of caste, is unheard of in Hindu society—especially in Dabbanda. In most villages, there are moments where the caste segregation lifts, particularly during festivals. But in Dabbanda, the castes had always stayed separate, even during holidays and feasts. Their faithfulness to division by castes was strict even by Hindu standards. Now, for the first time in hundreds of years, Dabbandans from different castes worship and eat and worship together because of Christ's work. God has done more miracles in Dabbanda than raising the dead and healing the sick.

The Christian community in Dabbanda is growing, and the Hindus have become concerned that the Christian population might soon outnumber the Hindu community. Although many of the Dabbanda Christians have been forced to relocate to find jobs, the number of baptized believers has doubled. "This is the Lord's doing; it is marvelous in our eyes" (Psalm 118:23, KJV).

11

Ordinary Preachers

In order to plant churches that are strong in love, empowered by the truth of the Gospel, and saturated in Scripture, pastors must first be equipped to lead those churches and know the Bible for themselves. Since most will be walking into communities that have virtually no understanding of God's word or God's will, they must be able to teach and explain Christ clearly.

The Discipleship Training Center was created for exactly that purpose. And John David was one of the first and brightest products of Love-n-Care's DTC.

Yet most people would not have predicted a bright future for John David as a child. Although he was born into a relatively wealthy, middle-class family, his father was an alcoholic who didn't spend much time with the family. When he did, he clearly favored John David's older brother. Since his mother's favorite was the youngest son, John David was left out. His parents would take his brothers out to town, leaving him at home, and would buy them new clothes, giving him hand-me-downs. He felt the rejection deeply, and he grew to hate his family for their coldness to him. In fact, by the age of five, his parents left him to his grandparents' care.

Abandoned by those who should have loved him best, John David somehow retained a sensitive nature. He was deeply interested in the spiritual world, and began visiting the Hindu temples and asking questions about the different gods. When he was a little older, he broadened his search and began investigating the Muslim mosques. But ultimately it was pleasure and popularity that won his heart, and he began to pursue the idols of the world. Although his guilty conscience plagued him about the sinful choices he was making, the bad friends he loved, and the gang he had become involved in, he was a slave to his rebellion. He wanted to be a better person, but he was unable to find the way out of his sin.

God had to call John David many times before he heard. When complications from a botched operation left him close to death, a pastor came and prayed for healing. Although John David was restored to health the very next day, he hardened his heart.

Then there was the little girl he tutored. She was only nine years old, running to his house every day after school in her faded school uniform. Every day, before they began, she bowed her dark head to ask Jesus to bless her as she studied. John David began to mock her. "How can you worship without a god in front of you?" he would laugh. Yet the serious little girl wasn't afraid of his taunts, and she shared the reality of Christ instead. She even invited him to a Christian revival meeting, and told him he ought to go and get prayed for.

Like Yesupadam, John David found himself going to a revival he didn't even want to attend. And like Yesupadam, John David was convicted to the point of repentance. Against his will he found himself weeping uncontrollably over his sin, asking God for the reconciliation through Jesus that leads to life. Receiving that forgiveness, John David was flooded with irrepressible joy. He stayed up all night just to talk with his Lord, and although he had never felt skilled at praying, he felt this time that he was talking with his most intimate friend. He was a changed man at the age of sixteen.

His friends couldn't believe the change in their once morose and somber friend who now smiled from ear to ear and told them about his new love for someone named Jesus. They couldn't imagine why a teenager who used to dabble in many religions, visiting mosques and temples with equal interest, would now devote his life so totally to the Christian God. "John David," one of them finally asked, "what are you so excited about? Is it your birthday or something?"

"No, it's not my birthday," John David began, but then changed his mind. He began laughing again, and said, "Well, I guess it is!"

He had truly changed, and God had much in store for him. In February of 1995, some men from Love-n-Care Ministries came to his hometown of Guntur. His hungry soul was eager to hear more about Christ, and he decided to investigate. But he immediately dismissed the group after he saw the white men who were traveling and preaching with Yesupadam. He assumed that they were the stereotypical, selfish imperialists who wanted to make money rather than help the people of India. He had grown up with a deep suspicion of internationals—especially white people—and he concluded that these men must be like others he had known. But somehow, despite his misgivings, John David found himself going to the evening meetings of worship and preaching. As Yesupadam spoke, John David was cut to the heart. He had criticized the pastors for being self-serving, and yet Yesupadam was exhorting him to change from *his* selfish ways and share his life in Jesus with the lost in India.

Convicted, John David responded at once to God's reproof, and went forward to pray. He began, "God, I submit my entire life to you. I will serve you however you want, all the time. My life is all yours."

The pastors surrounding him began to pray as well, but with a slightly more specific emphasis: "Thank you Lord, for calling this man into full-time ministry!"

John David had not realized before that God might be drawing him to such a ministry, and their prayers surprised him. But as he continued to offer himself to God, their words began to ring true in his heart. "Yes, Lord," he prayed. "I am here. Wherever you want me to go, I will go."

Impressed by the integrity, sincerity, and passion of the pastors from Love-n-Care Ministries, John David quickly realized that "wherever you want me" was in Visakhapatnam with Yesupadam. After he spent ten days in prayer and fasting, this sense was confirmed by the Holy Spirit, calling him to join LNC's Discipleship Training Center. John David felt strongly that he was supposed to go immediately, even though that would mean going empty-handed.

When he went to tell his mother (who was herself a new believer) about his decision, she was not happy. "Please don't leave me now," she pleaded. "Why don't you wait until after I die, and you have no reason to stay here? You don't have to go now, do you?"

But John David was resolute. "Mother," he replied, "I know that you love me. But the love of Jesus is even stronger than your love. I have to obey him first. And that means that I have to go to Visakhapatnam."

He sold everything he had, and boarded a train for Vizag on March 31, 1995. He brought the clothes on his back and his Bible. Nothing else—not even shoes for his feet. He arrived at 5:30 a.m., searching for a ride to the ministry. He had five rupees in his pocket, but he had dedicated that money to give to LNC, so he prayed for another way. "God," he prayed, "please get me to Love-n-Care. I want the rest of my money to go to the mission. Please provide a way for me." Opening his Bible, he found a brochure for LNC with Yesupadam's phone number. Yesupadam answered the phone, and John David introduced himself.

"Are you coming to join the ministry?" was Yesupadam's first question. When John David said yes, he immediately replied, "Okay. I'll be right there to pick you up."

With that, John David enrolled in the Discipleship Training Center. Once he had given his gift of the little money he had, he stood empty-handed, having nothing except for a strong desire to learn and be equipped for the work of the Gospel. For a year, he had no change of clothes. He didn't even have a towel, until someone else in his class lent him one. But his heart was full of the joy of the Lord and he did not feel in any way deprived.

* * *

Each year, dozens of men and women like John David come to the Discipleship Training Centers. Many are young believers. Most are quite poor. All come with a desire to know God more fully, and to be trained to impact their nation with the message of Jesus Christ. The DTC is an intensely focused and pragmatic program for men and women who desire to be placed in ministry in some capacity. Because many of these students go to rural villages or tribal areas, the program focuses on core Biblical teachings and direct application rather than some of the more complex points of theology. Although the curricula may vary from year to year, the core subjects are:

- Church planting
- Practical discipleship
- Communion with God
- Conflict resolution
- Evangelism
- Faith
- The cross of Christ
- New life in Christ
- Old and New Testament surveys
- Pastoral epistles

Recently, with an influx of teaching from Western pastors, the DTC has invested more time in the basic foundations of systematic theology. Teaching about the important themes of the Bible has helped ground the students in the essentials of Scripture. Even these newer additions to the curricula, however, are intended to equip a future pastor or leader with practical tools for teaching about and growing in Christ. Love-n-Care Ministries is focused on training disciples, not academics. As Yesupadam says, they are raising up a small but mighty "Gideon's army" of believers to impact their nation with the precious truth of the Gospel.

Teaching this group of students is no easy task. The students come from very different backgrounds, and the DTC teachers have to find ways to make the material they teach accessible to every student in the class. University students sit next to illiterate day laborers at the Discipleship Training Center. This means that, before they can even study the Bible, some of the students have to learn to read. Some come from comfortable middle class backgrounds, and others have been involved in gangs or lives of crime. The students also come from varied spiritual backgrounds, and experienced Christians are enrolled with relatively new believers. Some of the students even arrive at the school unbaptized, which carries significant meaning in Indian culture. In India, many people profess to trust Christ after hearing a Gospel presentation, but it is not until a person is baptized that he or she is recognized as a strong and dedicated believer. These unbaptized students, who may be wavering in their faith before they come, are baptized during the school year as they become more convinced of the reality and urgency of Christ's call on their lives.

Although teaching such a diverse group of students is quite a challenge, it is consistent with Love-n-Care's philosophy of ministry. They are not looking only for the bright and talented. Instead, they seek to equip everyone who has a desire to minister to the body of Christ. Some, like John David, end up overseeing large portions of the ministry. Some pastor a small church in a simple rural village. Some cook hundreds of meals for the Children's Home. Some devote their lives to intercession. Others teach in the school. But all are involved in the work of ministry. All are disciples of Christ.

This perspective on ministry has had a profound impact on people like Kiran, a slender man with an exuberant, happy-go-lucky personality and an obvious love for people. Because he had attended a Bible college before he came to Love-n-Care Ministries, Kiran initially resisted going to the DTC. He saw no need for another year of training, and he wanted to get involved in ministry right away. However, the leaders encouraged him to study with them, and so Kiran entered the class of 1992. He was surprised to discover that it was a very different experience from his education at the Bible college.

"I learned the meaning of true discipleship at the DTC," Kiran says. "I received strong correction there, which was something I did not get at the Bible college. The college taught the Bible, but they didn't talk about our personal lives. Here at the DTC, heart attitudes and personal lives are very important."

Kiran had experienced little in the way of personal accountability at the Bible college, and he was left to his own devices when it came to application. As a result, Kiran had returned to some deeply-rooted sins from his unbelieving past. No one asked him the tough questions about how he was living his personal life, and so although Kiran knew his old habits were displeasing to God, he felt helpless to change. At the DTC, however, he was given the help and accountability he needed to break his bondage to sin. After Kiran confessed the patterns of sin in his life, Yesupadam reproved him sternly. It was hard to take at first, but Kiran soon realized that it was God's gracious way of dealing with sin. In a way, DTC was a breaking experience for Kiran, but he found that his brokenness opened him up to receive the hope of God's forgiving and renewing grace.

"Changing my life and my heart attitudes was very difficult," Kiran says. "But at the same time, I was shown the holiness and the love of God. The DTC teachers showed us the whole Word of God. That was also the first time in my life that I ever received true encouragement. I told Yesupadam that I was but dust. I didn't feel like a talented person, and the teachers at the Bible college had always focused on the gifted people. Yesupadam reminded me that God doesn't limit himself to the talented people. In fact, the Lord loves to use the weakest people so that the glory will go to him. Krupa and Yesupadam gave me so much encouragement while I was at the DTC."

Many others have had experiences like Kiran at the Discipleship Training Center. Although some things have changed since the first DTC class in 1991—students who formerly studied sitting on dirt floors in cramped, hot rooms now have benches to sit on and electric fans to stave off the stifling afternoon heat—much is still the same. "Our vision is to make disciples," said Krupa, the school's director, a charismatic man who speaks with great passion. "Jesus gave his vision to his disciples, and they carried it around the world. Our students are taking that vision to the lost in India. God is going to use our students in His kingdom, for His own purposes. Our job at the DTC is to make them flexible and useful for whatever work God brings to them."

The preparation is indeed intensive, although perhaps not as intellectually rigorous as many other programs. The school's schedule reflects their focus on practical application and a vibrant personal relationship with the Lord. DTC students wake up at 4:45, and spend an hour in corporate prayer before they return to their rooms for two hours of personal time for private devotions and daily preparations. Students spend another hour in prayer after chapel and breakfast. It is only then that they go to class and receive four hours of instruction. Afternoons are given to additional prayer times for the men, vocational training for the women, and outreach trips several times weekly. In the evenings, DTC students attend church events or prayer meetings in homes, and involve themselves in the work of the local church and ministry. "They are like the worker bees of Love-n-Care," Krupa said. "They fill in the gaps and provide for the unexpected needs of the ministry." In this Indian ministry, where no one knows what challenges will be around the next corner, people who can arise to meet any need are very valuable.

This practical emphasis is perhaps most evident in the April Tribal Camp, where the DTC students are sent out to apply the teachings they have received. At Tribal Camp, these men and women are given a wonderful opportunity to share Christ and intercede for the lost in their nation. Even more importantly, however, they are introduced to a mission field on which many of them will soon be asked to labor permanently, planting churches, nurturing believers, and testifying to the power of Christ in their lives.

The men and women who come to the DTC are not all the best and the brightest. Although most of them are strong Christians with a sincere and persistent passion to serve God, many come from difficult backgrounds. Some of them were alcoholics before they came to the DTC. Some have been possessed by demons. Others have dealt with sexual sins and perversions. A few were criminals. Although these men and women have a new life in them and a desire to change, indwelling sin and stubborn habits often resist growth. As a result, some of the students at the DTC undergo dramatic transformations over the course of their year at LNC. Although many of these life changes are difficult and slow, the Holy Spirit's power is sure and unstoppable.

Alexander was one such man who needed accountability and help to change. He had been a professional assassin before he became a Christian, and he had knifed several people to death. Because he was so accustomed to power and rebellious independence, he found submission to his God-given leaders very difficult. He also had a hard time settling disputes peacefully with his peers. At one point, Alexander became involved in a quarrel with another DTC student, and he became violently angry. Unwilling to quiet his anger, forgive his brother, or work for reconciliation, he grabbed the other man by the throat and held him in the air with his bare hands. Terrified, the student screamed for help. Other students came running to help, and rescued their friend. Krupa spoke to Alexander very sternly, reproving him for his sinful outburst of anger. After receiving conviction from Krupa and the Holy Spirit, this assassin who despised having to show respect and submission broke down in repentance, asking for forgiveness. His life was becoming a testimony of radical change.

The Discipleship Training Center is a place of intense effort for both students and teachers. About 30 per cent of the students are married men, many of whom leave their families for a year in order to complete the training. This is both financially and emotionally straining, and the ministry hopes to one day construct married student housing so the families can be closer. Love-n-Care Ministries funds all students, paying for their tuition, room and board, including students who come from other ministry groups. But the ministry cannot currently provide for families who are trying to make ends meet while a spouse is studying at the school. Although LNC tries to carry much of the financial burden, the families at home have to sacrifice in order to send their husbands and fathers off to school.

Even without the added concerns of a family, many of the single students face challenges of their own. Many students come with only a very few belongings, and it can be a hardship to make it through a year without money to buy clothes, soap, shoes, and other necessities. There are academic difficulties too, as it is difficult to find good materials in Telugu, and perhaps only 20% of the students can read an English translation. The center has Telugu Bibles, one Bible dictionary in Telugu, and a partial concordance for the school. It is a sparse library for so many students. More books and study materials are needed.

Yet the challenges that the DTC faces are small in comparison to the rich returns the school sees. The first DTC in 1991 was a small program of 12 students, and now the DTC in Vizag graduates between 20 and 40 students a year. About half of the students go on to work directly with Love-n-Care, but 95% of the graduated members are involved in some type of Christian ministry. There are now many hundreds of DTC graduates who have dedicated themselves to the work of Christ, and are serving in a myriad of ways across southeastern India. Their contribution is incalculable—and growing.

12

Just Like Elijah

Although the Discipleship Training Center in Vizag was growing and flourishing, Yesupadam believed that something more was needed. Sending plains-Indian pastors into the tribal areas was a good plan, but sending tribal pastors to the tribal areas was a better one. How could LNC raise up an army of tribal ministers to go to their own people?

It all started with John Frederic.

He was an upper-caste tribal man (even the tribal peoples live under their own separate caste system) from a powerful family in Paderu, one of the larger tribal towns. Good looking, though a little reserved, with a quick smile and the slightly broadened features of the tribal people, John Frederic had a lot going for him. But he threw all that away for the love of the bottle. He was addicted, and he brought his friends down with him in his spiraling alcoholism. Although his family had aspired to great things through him—they wanted him to be a lawyer—he opted for technical training to become a welder. Even there, however, he was unable to get a job. Guilt-ridden over his alcoholism and his family's honor, John Frederic became suicidal.

In the midst of those dark times, a few of John Frederic's Christian friends began explaining the peace of God to him. They told him that God was faithful and good, a protector of those who fear him. In desperation, John Frederic began to pray: "Jesus, if you are God, give me peace, and I will believe in you."

Several days later, John Frederic wandered into a church and sat down in the back to listen to the sermon. The preacher began sharing the story of Jesus' interaction with the woman caught in adultery. As John Frederic heard the story of Christ's compassion and forgiveness, he was overwhelmed. He began to weep as he heard Jesus' words to the woman: "Neither do I condemn you; go, and from now on sin no more," (John 8:11, ESV). At that moment, he confessed his sins to God and asked for forgiveness. John Frederic left the building as a new man. God had answered his prayer; he now had not only peace, but overwhelming joy in his life.

His family, however, were appalled when they found out that their son had been going to a low-caste Christian church. His parents had thought his alcoholism was bad, but in their minds, this was far more shameful. His father sat him down, hoping to talk him out of his foolishness. "Don't you know that everyone sees you spending time with those low-caste Christians?" he said. "You have brought dishonor on this family. If you decide to go to that church, don't think you can be part of this family too."

His sister had her own take on the situation. "Don't you know that no woman from our caste will marry you now?" she asked. "You could have had a good marriage, made a good match. You've thrown it all away to become a Christian."

But his father's threats and his sister's condemnations were unable to stop John Frederic. Although his living stipend was cut off and his family treated him like a stranger, he kept going to the church where he had found forgiveness and hope. In an Indian culture, and especially in a rural, tightly-knit tribal culture, family networks provide access to employment, housing, community acceptance, and marriage prospects. For John Frederic, it was intimidating to think of creating a livelihood without the support of his family. By giving up his family's connections and assistance, John Frederic stepped out in faith, trusting in the God he loved to provide for him.

Sensing that God was calling him to full-time ministry among his people, John Frederic became the first tribal man to attend Love-n-Care's DTC in 1993. After a year of training and a second year as an apprentice in Vizag, John Frederic felt a strong desire to return to Paderu. As he prayed, he felt God confirming his desire. But although he knew that he belonged in Paderu, he decided not to say anything. Instead, he began to pray, "God, if this is your will for me, have Yesupadam ask me to go to Paderu."

Toward the end of the year, Yesupadam took John Frederic aside. "I think you should go back to the tribal area," he said. "Will you go help Christopher with the tribal ministry in Paderu?" It was confirmed.

There was only one problem: John Frederic needed a wife to help him in his ministry, and he knew that his parents would never choose a Christian wife for him. Seeing John Frederic's problem, Yesupadam took it upon himself to play matchmaker. As a respected leader in the Christian community, Yesupadam often arranged marriages for believers, especially for those too poor to afford a marriage. Besides, he had someone in mind for John Frederic.

Yesupadam had noticed Priscilla, a quiet and beautiful young woman in John Frederic's DTC class. She was very intelligent, and quick to serve. She never complained, which made Yesupadam think that she might deal well with the challenges of the tribal area. Noticing her, he thought, "Priscilla and John Frederic would be wonderful together—both of them are so committed to the Lord and so eager to follow him." Besides, Yesupadam took great pleasure in thwarting caste and culture in the freedom of Christian marriage—John Frederic was a tribal man, and Priscilla was an untouchable.

Although Priscilla and John Frederic both agreed to Yesupadam's match and believed that the Lord wanted them to marry one another, John Frederic's parents were insulted when they heard that Yesupadam had acted for them, and they lashed out angrily at their son: "Who does Yesupadam think he is, and why should he be the one to arrange your marriage?" Priscilla's parents, who had been trying to arrange a marriage for Priscilla already, felt similarly offended. Ironically, the parents on both sides saw the match as an unfavorable one for their child. Untouchables consider themselves above tribal people, but high-caste tribal people see their class as superior to the "casteless" untouchables. Because of these prejudices, both sides of the family saw the marriage as beneath their rank in society. Ultimately, however, they gave in and allowed their children to marry. As a result, their marriage has become another testimony of the reconciliation found in Christ.

Over their three-month engagement, Priscilla and Frederic fell in love. Romance came as a surprise to them. Priscilla hadn't felt excited about the match when Yesupadam asked her about it, but after several months of praying, she decided to trust Yesupadam's wisdom. John Frederic hadn't felt much emotion about the prospect initially, but he too wanted to respect Yesupadam's insight. But after their engagement, John Frederic and Priscilla began to spend more time together, and a quiet love grew between them. She became intrigued by the passionate tribal man—so different from her—who was to become her husband. And John Frederic wasn't immune to her shy beauty and her faithfulness to God. After a simple wedding, the couple moved just outside Paderu.

Hidden deep in the mountains, Paderu doesn't feel like the jungle. Instead of the thick vegetation and tall palm trees found in the foothills, the steep hillsides are open and rocky. Old rice terraces form horizontal ridges across the mountains and shorter, scrubby trees and bushes cover the uncultivated areas. In the dry season the landscape feels brown and almost arid, but there is a unique beauty in the scattered boulders, resilient trees, and still paddies. The cool evenings were a surprise to Priscilla, used to the constant warmth of the lower altitudes. Growing up in an area where a 75 degree day in winter brought out wool shawls, earmuffs, and scarves, Priscilla was unprepared for the mountain weather that sometimes approached closer to 55 degrees at night. Yet the weather and the landscape were minor changes compared to the shock of tribal life. It was a good thing she had John Frederic, because at first she had no one else. Her new love for her husband helped Priscilla adjust to a difficult life and a strange culture. Although the pastors tried to prepare her for the tribal area, nothing could protect her from its challenges except the sustaining grace of God and her confidence that she was obeying His call.

It wasn't easy. Her parents-in-law did not accept her. The food was much spicier than what she was used to, and yet she had to eat it at every meal, day in and day out. Tribal men treat their wives differently than plains Indians do, so she had to adjust to a new code of gender relations. In addition to all of these things, they were in Christian tribal ministry, which meant poverty for the newlyweds. She and John Frederic came to Paderu with only a six-year old blanket and two small carpets for the church, both of which Christopher had given them. Nothing else. If Christopher had not also lent them a few cooking pots, they would not have even had anything with which to prepare food. But even this did not daunt Priscilla. "I knew that when I went to the tribal area, I would only have John Frederic and Jesus," she said. Truly, that was all she needed.

John Frederic and Priscilla received 400 rupees a month from Love-n-Care. It was barely enough to live on. They slept in the church—a small thatched hut—and cooked their meals over an open fire outside. When John Frederic's brother learned of their poverty, he bought them their own cooking pots and utensils. It was enough to scrape by.

Along with the poverty and loneliness came spiritual attack. Christopher, who was training John Frederic to lead the tribal ministry, had to leave after a year because of the Hindu threats on his life. Priscilla became very ill after the birth of their first child, and struggled to completely recover. One day, Frederic came home and found his wife pinned to her bed, attacked by evil spirits. Speaking to her in an audible voice, they said, "We are going to kill you and your husband." Feeling the power of God sweep over him, John Frederic ran to his wife's side, knelt on the ground, and began worshipping the Lord. Immediately, the spirits left.

Despite all these pressures, Priscilla resisted discouragement and continued to support her husband faithfully in the ministry. As a result, John Frederic's work in the tribal area began to bear fruit. With much boldness, he and the other Christian believers walked to the surrounding villages, proclaiming the love of God for those who repent and believe in His name. He learned to trust God to provide visible manifestations of his power for the uneducated, skeptical tribal villagers. He found God's faithfulness time and again. The tribal people believe when they see miracles, and so God provides miracles. Supernatural signs and wonders most often occur in individual healings, but sometimes God works to bless an entire village.

One such miracle happened in a larger village of about a hundred people, deep in the tribal mountains. It had taken all day to hike there, so the men decided to wait until morning to speak to the people. Thinking that John Frederic and the others were Naxalites (guerilla communist rebels), the village readily fed and sheltered them for the night.

As is their habit, the men went to the head elders in the morning, explaining who they were and why they had come. The village leaders were surprised to hear that the men were Christians, but since the strangers seemed to want to help the people, they gave their permission to speak anyway. The head elders called the rest of the village to the central clearing, and invited John Frederic and the others to speak.

Before they began sharing about Jesus, the men felt led to ask the villagers about their personal health and welfare. They soon discovered a universal, intense need: rain.

"We haven't had rain for a whole year," one man in the crowd volunteered. "Now there is no food for us. What can grow without rain?"

The rest of the gathering agreed silently, each tired face attesting to the strain of hunger and an uncertain future. Seeing their need, John Frederic was moved with compassion for them. And their circumstances reminded him of another drought long before.

"We are Christians," he said. "and we have come to tell you about the power and love of our great God. Let me tell you about a man of God named Elijah. Because of his people's sin, God commanded that no rain should fall for seven years. Because He controls the heavens and the earth, the sky obeyed Him and no rain fell. There was a severe famine in the land, because there was no water. But God did not simply want to punish His people—He wanted to show them His love.

"Elijah called for a test to prove who the real God was. He told the people, 'You cannot serve all of these gods. If these other gods are real, serve them. But if the Lord God is real, serve him only.' The people watched to see which god would send fire to the sacrifice.

The priests of the other god prayed, sacrificed, and beat themselves for hours, pleading for their god to accept their sacrifice. When the priests were exhausted, even they had to admit that nothing happened. To prove how powerful his God was, Elijah poured water on his sacrifice, and then asked God to burn it with fire. Immediately God sent fire on Elijah's sacrifice, at once consuming the sacrifice and the water all around it. The people watching were amazed, because they saw that only this God was real. They repented for worshipping other gods, and trusted in the true God.

"God's people had turned against Him to follow other gods. But now that they had repented and turned back to Him, He demonstrated his forgiveness and love. He is not a god who remains angry with those who ask for His mercy. In fact, the Bible says that He is 'slow to anger, and abounding in love and faithfulness.' He was quick to show that love and faithfulness to His people.

"Elijah told the people that it would rain. He told the king, his enemy, that it would rain. He went up on top of a mountain, and prayed. At first, nothing in the sky changed. Yet Elijah kept praying, and at last a small cloud appeared in the sky. He prayed again, and the clouds grew thick and dark. God sent a heavy rain to bring life back to the barren land.

"This is the same God we come to tell you about. He is the only true God, and you must not follow other worthless gods. Ask him to forgive you for obeying your idols, and He is quick to forgive. The power and love he demonstrated long ago is not just a story from the past—he is eager to show himself to you today."

Using the story of Elijah, John Frederic began to explain about Jesus, the ultimate expression of God's love and forgiveness. After showing them how to repent of their sins and trust Christ as their Savior, John Frederic asked them to demonstrate their faith.

"If you trust this God," he said, "kneel down right now, and we will pray together for rain. He did it for Elijah, and we believe that He will do the same miracle here. Kneel down and pray with faith in your Lord!"

About thirty men and women knelt in the red dust and began to pray. The village's idol priest was there. As he listened, his heart began to resonate with the words John Frederic spoke. Kneeling together with his neighbors and friends, he gave up his career, livelihood, and social status to trust in a God whom he now served not as a priest, but as a son.

John Frederic and the other men began walking among the thirty, anointing them with oil and praying with them. Although some of the thirty prayed for rain without submitting their lives to Christ, twenty men and women (including the priest) became

Christians that afternoon. Although their hope for rain had not been fulfilled, they were willing to trust in a God and Savior whom they already knew to be beautiful and true.

The next day, heavy rains fell.

* * *

In order to sustain and increase the effectiveness of Love-n-Care's tribal ministry, Yesupadam asked John Frederic to begin a Tribal Discipleship Training Center in 2000. This Tribal DTC has since made an essential contribution to the tribal ministry. Because tribal men are less educated and less wealthy than their plains Indian counterparts, very few were able to travel to Vizag and participate in the year-long program. Even though their own tuition and board would be covered, it was too much of a financial burden on their families to leave for a year. Besides financial pressures, the linguistic, cultural, and educational gaps were difficult to bridge. And yet, these tribal Christians desperately needed teaching about God's word, church-planting, and pastoring. They are the most effective missionaries to their own people, and they need discipling. It became clear that a Tribal DTC would multiply the ministry's ability to do evangelism, outreach, and church-planting among the tribal peoples.

Although the tribal believers usually have less knowledge, their commitment (once made) is full and unshakeable. Before they even become followers of Christ, they know the significant cost that is involved. In small, tightly-knit tribal villages, breaking with tradition to join the followers of Christ is a significant risk. Those who are still willing to become His disciples are single-minded in their devotion. This passion and commitment provides a fruitful environment for the DTC. The program is only six months long, with the teaching concentrated on the essentials of Christianity. John Frederic does all the training for the Center, so he carries a great burden. Most of these men go out to plant their own churches in the tribal area—challenging work by any standard.

Those who enroll in the tribal DTC have a unique schedule, suited to their needs. Because the Center is a streamlined program designed to train pastors rather than a variety of Christian workers, the classes are smaller and only for men. John Frederic teaches class in the morning, covering essential topics in the Bible in his 6-month condensed program. Because of the financial pressure most of these men face, afternoons are left free so that they can work to help support their families. In the evenings, the men gather again to participate in house prayer meetings, where they have opportunities to preach and lead prayer times.

In addition to these frequent prayer times, the first Wednesday of the month is designated for an all-night prayer meeting. When they are not attending these prayer meetings, they often spend their evenings in community outreach in their local neighborhoods. Thursdays are reserved for tribal outreach, hiking deeper into the more remote regions to preach in the villages. Once a month, ten to fifteen pastors and students head out for a week-long outreach mission, going farther into the interior to reach new villages in the tribal belt. By taking a full week for outreach, the pastors and students are able to cover a new area each month, hiking to villages deep in the mountains that range in size from only a few houses to villages of 500 or more.

The tribal DTC focuses on three main essentials: the Scriptures, evangelism, and prayer. In the courses John Frederic teaches, he equips the men to study the Word of God and interpret it carefully and accurately. Through their weekly and monthly outreaches, the DTC students are constantly reminded of the lost around them and have the opportunity to share the Gospel they love in meaningful ways. Perhaps one of the most obvious differences between western seminaries and the tribal DTC is the emphasis on prayer. The pastors in Love-n-Care Ministries view Christian work as fruitless without the essential work of prayer, and this priority is demonstrated in their schedules. Many of the Christians at Love-n-

Care spend hours in daily personal prayer, in addition to frequent corporate prayer. This emphasis is even more apparent in the tribal areas, where many Christians are illiterate or barely able to read, making individual Bible study difficult. Prayer then becomes the lifeline of faith.

Through the graduates of the tribal DTC, tribal ministry in LNC has exploded. When John Frederic became a believer in 1993, Love-n-Care had only one church in the tribal area. When he returned to pastor in 1995, there were five or six churches. In 2007, Love-n-Care was responsible for over 200 churches in the tribal area. But even this is only the beginning.

13

Let the Children Come

If you were to walk into the headquarters of Love-n-Care Ministries in Visakhapatnam, you might not immediately notice the offices, or Yesupadam sitting down to tea on the porch with a visitor, or the pastors walking to and from their business. In fact, you might not notice any adults at all. If you wandered into the walled-in courtyard on a hot Saturday afternoon, your attention would be arrested by over 200 children playing in the red dust. Many of the boys, running around with an old tire or creating some chaotic game in a blur of excited shouts and thin brown legs, would hardly notice you. But some of the quieter girls, playing rock games on the patio, might lift their dark eyes and smile shyly. If they knew you, their reserve would melt away, and the younger ones would flock to touch your hands and greet you with bright smiles. "Praise the Lord, brother! Praise the Lord, sister!" they would say. Although they play like ordinary children, their lives and godly devotion are extraordinary. These are the children of Bethany Children's Home, and their faith-filled prayers are the backbone of the ministry.

Yesupadam hadn't intended on including children in his ministry. Although God had led him to add children in the bylaws of the ministry, he hadn't then felt any desire to work with them. His passion was to share the Gospel with those who hadn't heard it, and he saw caring for children as something completely different. Yesupadam wanted to build churches. When he was visiting the U.S., he spoke to a Bible study in Vermont, where he was asked about the Indian children. To him, it seemed like a surprising question to ask an evangelist/church planter.

"I'm not interested in doing that," he said. "That's social work. I want to share the Gospel." But they urged him to pray about it, and he agreed. He brought the children of India before the Lord in prayer, and sought God's will regarding his involvement with them.

A few days later, while still in Vermont, Yesupadam felt a sudden heaviness on his heart. He began to weep uncontrollably, and he heard an audible voice speaking to him. "Bethany," the voice said. "Bethany, Bethany."

I know God is speaking to me, Yesupadam thought. *But I have no idea what he is trying to say to me. What does "Bethany" mean?*

Opening his Bible, he looked up Bethany, and found that it means "house of poverty." He read Luke 24:50-51, and saw that Jesus took his disciples to Bethany and blessed them there before he ascended. *Jesus blessed the poor,* he thought. *It was his mercy toward the poor that brings them to heaven. And so many of the people of India are definitely poor, financially and spiritually. Lord, do you want me to help those people?*

As he considered that thought, Yesupadam's mind flashed back to his own childhood. In his mind's eye he saw himself as a little boy, standing by the road in his village. He was watching a man eating a banana, and his stomach ached with hunger. Fixated on the man's precious food, Yesupadam longed for just a little piece of the banana. But the man did not notice the staring child, or if he did, he didn't offer any of his snack. Finishing the last delicious bite, the man tossed the peel on the ground and walked off. As soon as the man's back was turned, Yesupadam snatched up the peel and devoured it hungrily.

As he thought about his childhood memories, he began to understand what God was telling him. "Lord," Yesupadam said. "You are telling me about the children. You want me to have mercy on them. I can care for them physically and spiritually in a way that I was never cared for. Training the children isn't just social work. It is Gospel work."

When the believers in Vermont heard this, they were overjoyed. Each of them agreed to support a child, so Yesupadam called his wife on the phone.

"Padmini," he said. "Find seventeen children who need a home, and take them in. We are going to start a children's home, and some believers in the U.S. want to support them."

Padmini found twenty-five needy children, and Bethany Children's Home began in 1991. They rented a small house and began to feed and clothe them. When Yesupadam came back home a few months later, he looked in the window and saw the children eating their dinner. He began to cry as he watched their little hands scooping large handfuls of rice and curry from their tin plates. They were no longer hungry, and Yesupadam realized anew: *this is much more than social work.*

Children, however, require more than financial support. As the Home kept growing and more and more children needed Bethany's care, Yesupadam realized that he needed someone to take on responsibility of the children full-time. He needed someone who could love, direct, discipline, encourage, and train hundreds of children to love the Lord with all their hearts and souls (Deut. 11:13). It would take God's appointed person to care for so many children, and to care for them well.

That person was John David, and he was clearly gifted for the job. Even as a young man he had loved working with children. Although he is tall for an Indian and has an imposing presence and a resonant voice, his kindness and love for young people quickly puts people at ease. He first came to grips with the plight of India's children during an accidental interaction with a slum boy. Of course with God, there are no accidents.

A single man in his early twenties, John David was riding the train from Rajahmundry to Guntur one day when a young boy, about nine years old, caught his attention. He wore nothing but a small cloth around his waist. With one hand he held a broom, and with the other he smoked a cigarette.

"What are you doing with that cigarette?" John David asked him, rebuking him affectionately with a light smack on the back of the head. (Adults in India feel free to "parent" any children they see.) "You shouldn't be smoking that, especially at your age."

To John David's surprise, the boy cried out in pain. John David looked at his hand and saw blood. Dismayed, his stern rebuke melted into a rush of concern and compassion as he took the boy to the bathroom and examined his head. He had a large wound on the back of his head. It was several days old, stinking and oozing with pus. Gently John David cleaned out the wound, gave him some candy, and began asking the boy about his background.

He learned a lot in just a few minutes. The boy's father, a chronic drunkard, had been run over by a truck and killed in one of his drunken stupors. His mother had died before his eyes when her sari burst into flames as she cooked over her cooking fire. Although his grandmother had come to care for him and his sister, she was too old to do much. Facing starvation, Satish began cleaning train cars, hoping some passengers would pay him for his service. But the conductor found him on board without a ticket, and threw him from the train. Satish's head was wounded in the fall.

Giving the boy more candy, John David began to explain Jesus' love. "Jesus is the true God," he said. "He loves you, and even though your parents are dead, Jesus can be like a parent to you. He loves you that much."

Filled with concern for the boy, John David felt prompted to say more. "If you want, you can come home with me," he said. "I'll feed you and put you in school."

"I can't," Satish muttered. He didn't explain why.

Although John David was just a single college student with barely enough money to meet his own needs, he pressed further. "Bring your sister and grandmother. I'll take care of them too." But Satish still refused.

When John David got off the train at Guntur, he saw Satish again. Once more, he offered his home, and this time, Satish said yes.

John David took Satish to a restaurant and ordered him a meal. Tears welled up in his eyes as he saw how ravenously the boy stuffed the food into his mouth, as if he were afraid it might disappear if he left it on his plate too long. He took him to the hospital for his wound, and bought him some clothes—the first decent clothes he'd had in a long time. Satish lived with John David in his tiny college room, and John David began telling him about Jesus, teaching him songs that would remind him of who Jesus was.

One day, Satish fell ill with a very high fever. John David anointed him with oil and began to pray with great faith, believing that the Lord would heal the boy. But nothing happened. Distraught and confused, John David began to pray again.

"Lord, you have taken this boy's mother and father. Now do you want to take this child as well?" John David began to weep. "Why do you want to do this? Oh Lord, have mercy on this boy!"

Suddenly, John David was filled with a confidence that God was going to heal Satish.

"I declare healing in the name of Jesus!" John David said. Immediately the boy rolled on his side, vomited, and fell back, unconscious. John David took his wrist and felt for a pulse, but he couldn't find one. His heart tightened with fear, thinking the boy was dead. But then John David felt a peace, knowing that God had healed him.

After a minute or two, Satish opened his eyes, and his fever was gone.

As John David continued to pray and care for Satish, he felt the Lord telling him that he was to be the father of those children who didn't have parents. So he began visiting the railway stations, teaching the children like Satish about Jesus. There were so many.

"They are children of fear," John David says of those children. "Some of them have run away from home. Some have been abused; some are neglected. If the police find them, they will be put in jail. Others take advantage of these vulnerable children, bringing them into child-gangs, forcing them to beg, abusing them and taking the money from them. Some parents use their children to beg for the family, capitalizing on their pathetic and lonely appearance. Some even disguise their children to look like cripples, teaching them to lie so they can get more money. They are street-hardened children, but so many of them have hungry hearts. When I tell them about Jesus and His love, many are eager to give their lives to Him."

John David had demonstrated a heart for children throughout his life, but when he came to the Discipleship Training Center at LNC, he felt the time had come for him to minister to the unreached people groups in the tribal areas. He wanted to go preach to those who had never heard about Jesus, and he thought that his days of children's ministry were over. At the end of his year of training, he talked with Yesupadam about going to the tribal area.

"John David," said Yesupadam, "I know you would like to go to the tribal area, but we want you to stay and work with the children. We already have forty children here, and the numbers keep growing. We need someone to train them in the Lord, and you are gifted with children. If you go to the tribal area, you will touch a few lives. But if you stay here and work with the children, you will raise up a generation of evangelists to impact India. Pray about it."

It was a hard word of advice for John David to hear. He had wanted so badly to go to the tribal areas. But Yesupadam was not a man to be taken lightly. He was like a father to John David, even looking the part with his now thinning hair and glasses.

Yesupadam's sense of responsibility for the ministry lends him a powerful authority and provokes great respect from those around him. Both mentor and father figure to those around him, Yesupadam is not afraid of bringing stern rebukes and difficult words to the men and women he lives and works with. Yet the powerful love and affection he feels for those same people is abundantly evident as well. He is a man who carries the burdens of those around him, who displays a kind gentleness along with his authority.

So although John David wrestled with Yesupadam's counsel, his respect and love for his pastor and friend made him think more seriously about this new proposal. As he prayed, John David realized that God was giving him peace about following Yesupadam's recommendation. So he stayed with the children. At first he struggled with his assignment, because he longed to go out to the tribal areas, but as God began confirming his ministry to the children, he realized that Yesupadam's words were true. Through John David's leadership, Love-n-Care is raising up hundreds of passionate, courageous, and evangelistic young missionaries for the next generation. Even as children, they are bringing families, neighbors, and friends to Christ... and their work is just beginning.

The need for loving, Christ-centered training is painfully obvious in India. Half of India's population—550 million—is under the age of 14, which means that many of these children are growing up without an older generation to care for them. In fact, over 25,700,000 of those children are parentless.[5] That number is sharply increased by children with only one parent, and children whose parents cannot financially support them. There are thousands of children in desperate need of a home, and there could be no better environment than a Christian one for them. If India is to be reached for Christ, a significant thrust of that effort must be centered on the children.

Most of the children at Bethany Children's Home have lost a parent, sometimes both. Some have parents who were unable to care for them. Some others are children of LNC pastors. A few have been rescued from prostitution rings. Approximately 60% of the children come from Christian backgrounds, while the other 40% are Hindu. Most of the children who come from Hindu backgrounds give their lives to Christ after hearing about Him at Bethany.

John David hopes to reach more of the poorest of the poor—the rag pickers, the beggars, and the starving. Unfortunately, it is very difficult to get to those children. Lost among the alleys and bustling streets of India's cities, such children are thrust prematurely into adult lives. Often mistrustful of adults, the children who need help the most are usually unwilling or unable to seek out a stable life from strangers. They have too often been abused through misplaced trust. John David hopes to become increasingly effective in finding such children and winning their confidence. One day he hopes to set up day-care centers in the poorest slums and poverty-stricken villages, in an effort to reach those needy children.

Although only a minority of the children at Bethany come from backgrounds of abject poverty, all are still quite needy. Most of them have no ability to understand the wealth of the Western world. To these children, eating meat consistently or having a washing machine or more than two pairs of shoes are the subjects of wild fantasy. Many had never eaten three meals a day on a consistent basis before they came to Bethany Children's Home. John David remembers observing one boy who always gave his curry (a dish of meat or vegetables in spiced sauce) to his neighbors, eating only his rice. He never complained about it, but neither would he eat the vegetables.

"What are you doing?" John David asked him one day, upset at his wastefulness. "That curry is for you, to make you strong and healthy. Why aren't you eating your food?"

The boy lowered his head and muttered something unintelligible. Sensing that something was wrong, John David sat down, gave him a hug, and asked him to explain.

He soon discovered that the boy's parents had been too poor to buy vegetables or spices, so he had grown up on plain rice. When he tried to eat the curry, his undernourished stomach revolted, and he would vomit. Slowly, John David was able to introduce nutritious food into his diet so that he could eat good meals.

Although some parents find it difficult or impossible to care for their children, the cost is minimal by Western standards. In June, at the beginning of the school year, Love-n-Care Ministries provides each child with school uniforms, shoes, bags, and books—for the cost of about 2,000 rupees each ($10 US). If the parents can afford it, they are asked to provide 200 rupees ($1) for books, and about 60% of the parents are able to fund that expense. It only costs about 200 rupees ($1) a month per child for food. Their other expenses are negligible, since the 200 children in Vizag are kept in two large rooms—one for girls and one for boys. They sleep on blankets spread out on the concrete floor, and don't require pillows or other bedding. Their food is simple, but healthy. Most meals consist of rice and some sort of vegetable curry. Once a week, the children receive a hardboiled egg, and about once a month they get a meat curry. Recently an American church offered to provide one dairy serving per child per day. Because of their generosity, all the children receive yogurt with their evening meal. This has been a huge blessing, making the children's diet much more balanced. To most Western children, eating the same sort of food every day, sharing a room with a hundred other kids, sleeping on the floor, and owning only a small suitcase-worth of personal belongings would seem like a hardship. But coming from such destitute backgrounds, even these simple provisions are a huge blessing for the children who live at Bethany.

The Children's Home is meeting very real physical needs, but the primary purpose of the ministry is to provide spiritual care. The children receive intense, practical Christian training, and this emphasis is reflected in their schedule. The older children rise at 4:30 a.m. to pray, and the younger children wake at 5:00 am to do the same. From 6:00 a.m. to 7:00 a.m. they have time for personal devotions. Only then do they get to go eat breakfast, which is followed by a half-hour chapel time, where the children worship, pray, and receive a short teaching from the Scripture. They are at school from 8:30 a.m. to 3:30 p.m., and they study and do homework from 3:30 p.m. to 5:00 p.m. The children have only one hour of rest/play time per day. After dinner they have an hour of prayer in their respective rooms, and the younger children are in bed by 9:00 p.m. The older children study for another hour and are in bed by 10:00 p.m. Saturdays are special days, because the children only go to school for half a day, and get to play outside for a few hours in the afternoon. The teenage children have a special meeting with John David and the other children's workers, and Saturday evenings are reserved for co-ed prayer. In all, the children spend three hours a day in prayer and Bible study, and only one hour a day playing—a significant difference from most other children!

Yesupadam is fond of saying, "The prayers of the children are the backbone of our ministry." Early on, the children at Bethany learn that their prayers play a role of vital importance for the kingdom of God, and even the youngest children (usually three or four years old) are expected to participate in prayer times. Besides their daily prayer schedule, the children participate in monthly all-night prayer meetings. Some of the children fast on this day, too, although this is not required. In India, Christians pray in a different style than many Westerners do, and the way they pray encourages active participation at an early age. One person will lead in prayer, telling the rest what to pray for, giving a brief explanation of some specific need or issue. After his prompt, everyone begins praying aloud at once. Thus, prayer meetings in India are not quiet, orderly affairs, but active, noisy events in which everyone is called to pray simultaneously. Because of this, the children learn early on that they don't need to wait until they're older to be powerful in prayer. With simple, sure faith, the children at Bethany are convinced that their prayers are heard by a heavenly Father who loves to answer them. They are often reminded about the effectiveness of persistent, faith-filled prayer, and they understand the contribution of their prayers to the ministry's effectiveness.

Although many other children couldn't (and perhaps shouldn't) keep up with such a schedule, the children at Bethany Children's Home are remarkably well-trained. They are kept in large groups and have little individual time with adults, yet the children are very responsive, respectful, and obedient. The adults who oversee these children have noticed that their obedience and respect is consistent and genuine. In fact, many of the parents comment on the changes they see in their children when they come home on holiday. Having learned, "You shall love your neighbor as yourself" (Matt. 22:39, NASB), Bethany children are consistently more focused on others. And although they live in a large room with about a hundred other children, sleep on a concrete floor with a thin blanket, have only a handful of personal possessions, and eat very simple food, the children at Bethany seem to have a consistent joy and contentment that many more privileged children lack. Blessed with a stable environment and a confidence that God knows them and cares for them even when others can't, the children at Bethany have an unusual peace.

John David also makes sure that these children—some of them new believers—see themselves as active missionaries, even to adults. Before they leave on holiday to visit their families, John David reminds them of the importance of the Gospel and encourages them to share their new life with their friends and families when they go back home. Every year, the children return with stories of God's activity through them.

"These children are very brave, very courageous," John David says. "They confront the idol worship in their communities. They speak out and challenge the people around them, not just their own families. Many come back with stories of children who have received Jesus, and people who have been healed because of their prayers. Some parents have even become believers as a result of their child's testimony. When they come back from holiday, they turn in reports about their experiences. I am often amazed—the Holy Spirit gives them a miraculous wisdom to respond to unbelievers that many adults don't have."

Most people would probably consider Bethany a successful project already, but John David has been eagerly praying for more opportunities to minister. Currently there are five childrens' homes in Love-n-Care—the main home in Visakhapatnam and four others scattered around the region. All in all, Love-n-Care oversees about 500 children. John David would like to start three more children's homes in other cities with Love-n-Care churches. He hopes to open day-care programs in the inner cities and poorer villages. Rather than being just a place for working mothers to drop off their children, these day cares would provide malnourished, neglected children with a bath, a meal, and some educational training. Starting inner-city day programs is an ideal way to reach the poorest of the poor children.

Besides these goals, John David hopes to provide for some other, smaller needs. One day LNC would like to build a playground for the children, who currently play in a large, empty courtyard of red dirt. Ideally, John David would like to be able to provide separate rooms for each class, so that the children could have more individual attention from their caregivers. One day, he hopes to provide simple cots and bunk beds for the children, so that they don't have to sleep on the floor. Even these basic items would require more funding than the Home currently has. But the God who raises the dead and calms the seas also cares for the needs of small children, and John David has faith that the Lord will provide what they need. He always has.

What started out as an idea from a group of Vermont believers has now blossomed into one of Love-n-Care's most important ministries. Through the children raised at Bethany Children's Home, a new generation of Indians will be reached with the Gospel. Whether they grow up to be doctors, mothers, businessmen, teachers, engineers, or pastors, these children have learned that their doorstep opens onto a vast mission field. And because of John David, Yesupadam, and the rest of the workers at Bethany Children's Home, they have learned and experienced some of the riches of the fullness of Christ.

14

Hands of Mercy

The street that leads to Love-n-Care Ministries is a relatively quiet one, running past stands of tall palms and houses painted in bright tropical colors. Although Visakhapatnam is a coastal city, the ministry is situated in a colony in the hillsides above. Visitors who expect India to be arid and dusty are surprised by the lush hillsides surrounding the headquarters, and the beautiful flame-of-the-forest, a tree with bright orange blossoms that hangs over the walls of many enclosed courtyards. Although P.M. Palem Colony lacks the chaos of the urban areas, there is still plenty going on. Herders walk through the streets with a group of ugly water buffalo, women pass by with huge containers balanced delicately on their heads, and the daily jumble of wagons, motorcycles, cars, trucks, buses, pedestrians, and goats speaks of a thriving community going about its daily life.

Love-n-Care can look much the same at times—deceptively quiet. The wide dirt yard and tall whitewashed buildings can seem quiet on a hot afternoon, with electric fans pulling a little breeze into the offices, kitchen, and dormitories. Yet even on a quiet day, there are little hints of the bustle within—a polio amputee hobbling to the kitchen on his stick, getting a late lunch from the kitchen, the murmur of a prayer meeting in the church, a phone call in the office, news of an operation at the hospital, schoolgirls giggling and chatting as they squat on the ground with cutting tools between their feet, slicing vegetables for the hundreds they will feed at dinner. Without fanfare, Love-n-Care is doing the work of bringing practical help and the love of Christ to those in need.

Although Yesupadam had originally wanted to limit Love-n-Care ministry to tribal ministry and church planting, the opening of Bethany Children's Home began a flood of other mercy ministry opportunities. These mercy ministries, although requiring significant administration, time, and effort, are a great joy. There are so many needs, and each one that is met is a fulfillment of Christ's heart for the weak.

S.I. Samuel was a movie theater owner, the son of a police officer, and a Hindu. Because of "Bollywood" (the Indian movie industry, based in Bombay) and the popularity of movies, running theaters is a very lucrative (and respected) business in India. But at the age of forty, S.I. Samuel heard about Jesus. When he accepted Christ, his relatives disowned him and threw him out of the family. He learned immediately the cost of following Christ, but he remained faithful to God in the midst of his trial. Forced out of his home and his business, he began to preach about Jesus, traveling around the region to pastor believers and preach the Gospel to the lost. He was an uncompromising servant of Christ who walked closely with the Lord. As a result of his faith, Samuel was imprisoned, beaten, thrown into the drainage sewers, and left to die. Yet he kept preaching. At one point, traveling through the jungle at night, Samuel met with a tiger. Terrified, Samuel assumed that his earthly life was finished. He prayed for peace and safety. To his amazement, the tiger simply walked beside him peacefully, as if it were sent to guard him as he traveled. Samuel was a man of great faithfulness and confidence in his God.

One afternoon, S.I. Samuel came to visit Yesupadam. Samuel had visited Yesupadam many times as he traveled, but at the age of eighty, Yesupadam could see that he was getting older and weaker. This time, however, Samuel came with a request.

"Brother," Samuel said. "Can I stay with you? I am getting too old to keep traveling, but I have nowhere to stay."

Yesupadam was shaken. Sitting before him was a mighty man of God who had served the church for forty years with his care and encouragement. Yet here, as an old man, he had nowhere to rest, and no family to take him in. It broke Yesupadam's heart to see that no one else was being faithful to this steadfast man of God.

Taking S.I. Samuel into his home opened his eyes to a new area of need. One day, as he was praying, Yesupadam heard the Lord speak to him. "Son," he said, "take in others like Samuel. Serve them the way they have served the church—sacrificially and selflessly. These men and women have served me single-heartedly, without thinking about their own personal interests. Give them a place to rest."

So S.I. Samuel was the beginning of the Linton Old Age Home in 1995. It was built in Pithaparum, as a refuge for aging men and women who had served the Lord faithfully and were now destitute, a place for them to breathe their final breaths in peace. A Bethany Children's Home was also started in Pithaparum, so that the children could benefit from the wisdom of the older Christians, and so the aged could experience the joy of having grandchildren. Instead of having to live on the streets, these elderly believers are surrounded by exuberant young children in a stable, comfortable environment. For Love-n-Care Ministries, the Old Age Home is a way to show their gratefulness to those who have sacrificed everything for the Gospel.

Yet in India, it is not only the old who are helpless. One of the most shocking sights in India is the abundance of disabled beggars. The polio victims are some of the most heartbreaking figures, most of them missing one or more limbs because of the ravages of disease. Although polio vaccines have wiped out the problem in most industrialized countries, India continues to struggle with this deadly-but-treatable virus. In 1988, India had 250,000 cases of polio—70% of the world's polio patients. By 2001, because of vaccinations, this number had dropped down to 268. Although it seems miniscule in comparison to the 1988 figure, India is still home to over half of the world's new polio cases.[6] Progress in stamping out the disease, however, does not solve any problems for those who have already been afflicted with it. Polio frequently results in paralysis, usually to the lower limbs, but can occasionally cause quadriplegia.[7] Thousands upon thousands of Indians have been disabled by polio over the years. Without the ability to walk and work as manual laborers, these men and women are often reduced to begging. Opportunities for these unfortunate are few and far between.

That is where Love-n-Care has stepped in. The local government had observed LNC's work with the underprivileged, and in 2000 they asked the ministry to help.

"You do so well with people," the officials insisted to Yesupadam. "We need you to help with the polio victims. We'll fund the project if you'll help."

Although the government never acted on its promise to send funds, their request made Yesupadam think. Deciding that this was yet another opportunity to show Christ's compassion and love to the suffering, he decided to take up the project. He knew of no one else helping the polio victims, so Love-n-Care stepped in with a new Disabled Program.

Most of the students in the Disabled Program are in their late teens or early twenties—young people who are in an ideal stage of life to learn a new trade, but are inhibited by paralysis or amputation of one or more limbs. The ministry has several different vocational training programs—training in computers, printing presses, and tailoring. Each incoming student chooses one discipline to learn, and is trained accordingly. The students are given free food, free housing, free training, and free supplies during their instruction. In the future, Yesupadam hopes to provide them with whatever tools they need to become self-supportive after graduation. Although the program is one year long, some students take up to two years to complete their education (depending on physical and mental capacity). In 2004, about forty disabled students participated in the program.

The men and women in the program are not required to attend church services in order to receive their vocational training. However, nearly all of them do. As they observe the selflessness and joy of those in Love-n-Care, the disabled students become regular attendants at the children's morning chapel, Sunday school programs, church services, and prayer meetings. Every year, polio victims who have dedicated their lives to Christ are baptized along with new believers from the Children's Home, Junior College, and DTC. Unable to walk into the water themselves, the disabled students are carried into the water by an able-bodied friend. Their voluntary participation in the life of the church and ministry is a testimony to the powerful witness of the Christians who serve them.

Although training polio victims to be self-supportive is a critical work, it does not address the root problem: poor medical care. Good, accessible medical care is hard to find, even in a rapidly developing India. Although there are many excellent doctors, hospitals, and medical practices in India that offer cutting-edge medical knowledge and state of the art technology, those institutions are privatized and expensive. Public hospitals offer woefully insufficient care. In India's National Health Policy of 2002, the government admitted that in public medical facilities, "the equipment is often obsolete; the availability of essential drugs is minimal; the capacity of the facilities is grossly inadequate, which leads to overcrowding, and consequentially to a steep deterioration in the quality of the services." The same policy statement also noted that as a result, even those who can't afford private services refuse to go to public ones.[8] In fact, public hospitals are commonly thought of as places to go and die, rather than as places for healing. With so many people priced out of quality health care, and the general state of poor sanitation and ineffective disease prevention, even minor illnesses can become life threatening to the poor.

This is a problem that Love-n-Care is trying to change in its community. Affordable health care is a wonderful, practical way to show the love of Christ to a hurting population. This began with periodic medical camps run by Indian doctors willing to volunteer their time. Then in 1996, a doctor came to the ministry to run a clinic. Housed in a small one-room facility, the doctor attended patients daily, making do with his limited arrangements. However, neither occasional medical "blitzes" nor a lone doctor were able to fully meet the needs of the ministry and its community. There were so many needy people, and not enough time (or resources) to care for them all.

In 1999 a new hospital was built to address this problem. This medical center has provided much more advanced care for the needy. The Love-n-Care Hospital has a general surgeon, an OB-GYN physician, an ENT specialist, an orthopedist, an ophthalmologist, and a dentist on staff. These physicians volunteer their time so that the disadvantaged can come and receive health care. The hospital is equipped with an operating room, a laboratory, an x-ray room, a dental chair, a delivery room, and a pharmacy. Although small, this hospital has made specialized care affordable and regularly available to the community. It also provides a natural starting place for sharing the Gospel.

"Medicine and education are the two fields where people actually come to you for help," Yesupadam says.

But he isn't content to stick with a small, two-story hospital. The ministry has purchased the land and waded through the government red tape to get a new 100-bed hospital approved. It is currently being built, and its facilities will be equipped to care for a much greater number of patients.

In addition to these mercy ministries to the community, Love-n-Care is also busy with:

- A printing press and staff that translates and/or publishes books, tracts, and newsletters in Telugu, the region's primary language. The evangelistic tracts are taken on Tribal Camp missions and are sent to areas where personal evangelism has not yet taken place. By translating books into Telugu, Love-n-Care is making many valuable training materials available to their pastors and literate members,

- A Nursing School which provides medical/vocational training to those who want to pursue a career in nursing,

- A Computer Training School which equips students to understand and navigate some of the world's most important technology, and

- A Junior College which serves as a preparatory school for those in the community and Bethany Children's Homes who wish to go on to a degree-granting college or university.

Each of these ministries is designed to reach out to the community in ways that meet specific and legitimate needs. By caring for the physical, financial, and educational deficiencies experienced by believers and unbelievers alike, Love-n-Care is able to demonstrate real and practical love to those around them. Through their testimonies and their actions, the men and women who serve in this ministry are proclaiming the radical, sacrificial love of God, and the joy of new life that a relationship with Jesus produces. In the midst of a world of ever-present need, chaos, and desperate self-preservation, those who are "born of God" lead compassionate lives that demonstrate their life in Christ.

15

Blonde and Blue

Since the birth of Love-n-Care in 1990, Yesupadam had thrown his life into the ministry. His days were filled with training disciples, teaching and preaching, planning, and administrating the ministry—yet, his family life continued quietly in the midst of his hectic schedule.

Padmini was the source of Yesupadam's strength during the years following their conversion. Yesupadam's rebirth triggered a new life for both of them, and Padmini's relationship with the Lord flourished. Together, Yesupadam and Padmini were able to build a strong and stable marriage over the ruins of distrust, alcoholism, and depression. After her healing from breast cancer in 1984, she took on the role of helpmate to Yesupadam in a new way. She cared for his needs when he didn't take time to care for himself, and she trained the children to love and obey the Lord. She helped carry on the work of the ministry, taking on heavy responsibilities when Yesupadam traveled. She was a busy woman.

Although her efforts to nurture a healthy family and a thriving ministry were important, Padmini viewed her prayer life as her most important service. She spent long hours in prayer, praising God for his goodness and interceding passionately for those around her. Her prayer life was a natural extension of her love for others. Yesupadam often said that her prayers held the work of the ministry together. Before her conversion, Padmini had been faithful in the midst of desperation and disillusionment. But with the life of Christ within her, Padmini's grim perseverance bloomed into a joyful devotion to the Lord, her husband, and her family.

One evening in March of 1992, as Yesupadam and Padmini went for a walk, Padmini felt an excruciating pain shooting through her left hip. She was unable to move her left leg because of the pain, so Yesupadam had to pick her up and carry her home. The next day he took his wife to the doctor, who suggested a spinal scan. The test revealed that Padmini had advanced cancer in two of her lower vertebra. Sobered by the results of the tests, the doctors suggested that Padmini go to a larger hospital in Bombay. The prognosis did not look good, but with the limited equipment in Vizag, they were unsure of the cancer's spread. Only further tests could give an accurate prognosis for treatment.

A week later, Yesupadam and Padmini packed a few bags and boarded a train to travel across the country. At the Bombay hospital, Padmini was subjected to a new battery of tests. The strain on her frail body was too much, and Padmini's condition worsened rapidly. She was incapacitated by the pain, and Yesupadam had to carry her to and from the hospital. She was nearly paralyzed from the waist down.

When they returned to the hospital to get the results of the tests, the doctor was calm but pessimistic. "The cancer isn't limited to her spine," he told Yesupadam. "It has spread to her left hip, her right shoulder, and the right side of her brain. I'm sorry, but I don't think she will live for more than a few days. You'd better get her home as soon as possible."

Shaken, Yesupadam and Padmini left, trying to recover some semblance of order into their shattered world. In a matter of only a few weeks, Padmini had gone from planning a long future with her family to an imminent death sentence. Yesupadam was once again forced to face the prospect of life without his helpmate, lover, and friend. But in the midst of the waves of fear and uncertainty that threatened him, Yesupadam made a decision. "Lord, I trust you alone," he said. "You strengthen and comfort us, and You always bring good to your children—that includes Padmini, and it includes me. No matter what You do here, I will thank You for it."

They had been in Bombay for eighteen days, going back and forth from the hospital to the second floor of a church where they were staying. It had been exhausting for Padmini, yet she still had one more test before they could go home. But on April 7th, just 45 minutes before her appointment, she collapsed and stopped breathing. Yesupadam and his friend Devadas tried to find a pulse, but there was none. Her heart had stopped. Looking into her still, silent face, Yesupadam tried to grasp the fact that his wife was no longer with him.

Yesupadam and Devadas laid her body on the table, and then Yesupadam went downstairs to look for the pastor of the church. He wanted his friend to come and pray over Padmini. As he descended the stairs, he cried out to the Lord, "Oh God, I brought my wife all the way across the country to come here! She was sick, but at least she was still alive. How can I return home with a corpse?"

Only seconds later, Yesupadam heard Devadas shout from upstairs. "Yesupadam!" he yelled. "Yesupadam! Yesupadam!"

Startled into action, Yesupadam bounded up the stairs, wondering what could possibly be going on. Padmini's eyes were open, and she was asking for him. Rushing to her side, he grasped her hand and began rejoicing. "You heard my prayer, Lord!" he exulted. "You brought her back from the dead!"

Although still weak, Padmini was able to travel, so she and Yesupadam left Bombay the next day, beginning the 40-hour train ride home. But Padmini worsened again soon after they returned, and she was admitted to the hospital. Although the doctors were giving her chemotherapy and blood transfusions, nothing seemed to be helping. She could not eat or move. The doctors moved her to intensive care.

Yesupadam came to visit her on April 20th, but he quickly realized that he was not going to have an uninterrupted visit with his wife. The doctors were rushing around in her room, working furiously, and the nurses told her relatives to leave. He watched from outside the room, trying to see what was going on. Suddenly, all movement ceased and a new quiet filled the room. The nurses slowly began removing the various tubes connected to Padmini's body. They took the equipment out of the room, and the doctors left to file their reports.

They've given up, Yesupadam realized. *She's dead.*

He walked into the now-empty room and sat down beside her lifeless body. He began to pray, and as he spoke to the Lord, his prayer surprised even himself.

"Lord, I thank you for Padmini, for this precious woman you gave to me. You were so good to us! I know that you have taken her to be with you, and I know that I will see her again. There will be a wonderful reunion when my turn comes to be with you. Thank you for the hope that I can have in you."

Yesupadam continued to pray for about ten minutes. He prayed with his eyes open, looking at the form of his beloved wife. Then, an astonishing thing happened. He saw her eyes open.

"Yesupadam?" she asked. "Did you see me? Did you see me go up?"

Yesupadam could hardly believe his eyes, let alone answer her question. But he forced himself to remain calm. Gently, quietly, he replied, "What do you mean?"

"I died," she explained simply. "I felt myself passing through a very dark place. But then the darkness went away, and I knew that I was standing at the edge of God's glory. I couldn't see anyone, but I heard the most beautiful music. I wish I could explain what it sounded like. I couldn't understand the words, but it was wonderful. Yesupadam, I felt the presence of God like never before. I was so excited! I began shouting, *'Esay-ya!'* ('Jesus'), because I knew He must be coming there soon!

"But then it began to fade, and I began to come back here again. When I opened my eyes, I saw you sitting here next to me." Then Padmini smiled.

Still rejoicing in all that she had seen, Padmini threw off her covers and hopped nimbly out of her hospital bed. Paralyzed no longer, she began jumping up and down. Celebrating like a young girl, she was eager to demonstrate her restored body.

"Look! I'm healed!" she said excitedly. To prove it, she sat down on the floor, and then hopped back up again. "It doesn't hurt!" she laughed.

The doctors and nurses, looking through the windows of the ICU to see a dead woman jumping up and down, rushed back into the room. They just stared at Padmini.

Realizing that she had their attention, Padmini proclaimed, "Doctors! Look! Jesus has healed me!" And she continued jumping, sitting, and standing.

Shocked into speech, the doctors and nurses began to agree with her. "Your God must be a great god!" they said. They were face to face with the testimony of this obviously living woman, and God's revelation of His power in Padmini was inescapable.

Returning home to her husband and children, Padmini resumed her life, and for two years was unhindered by her cancer.

In May of 1994, however, her symptoms returned. As her health deteriorated, Padmini was confined to her bed, and the pain forced her to lie only on her left side. Despite her illness, she continued her ministry of prayer.

In early June, she called Yesupadam to her bed. Her voice was urgent, and her eyes pleaded with her husband.

"Yesupadam," she said, "God's people are called to be zealous like him, aren't they?"

"Yes," he replied.

"And you are a zealous servant of God?"

"Yes," he said again, wondering where her questions were going.

"Servants of God 'upset the world,' like Acts 17:6 [NASB] says, right?" she pressed.

"You are right, that's what it says," he answered.

"And Acts 24:5 says that such believers are 'troublemakers' [NIV], aren't they?"

"They are," he said.

"Yesupadam, you must be that kind of man." Padmini's eyes searched his as she spoke. "I want you to be a zealous servant of God, a man who will upset our world, and cause trouble—holy trouble. I've felt such a burden to tell you this all morning, and God is the one who is enabling me to tell you now. Don't be afraid of that responsibility. Don't worry about the consequences, and don't be afraid of doing it without me. I don't want you to yearn for me. God will go with you." As she finished, she sank back on her bed, exhausted with the effort of conveying her exhortation.

Padmini knew that this time, the Lord was finally calling her home, and she was right. Four days later, after praying with her husband, she closed her eyes and was gathered up to be with her Savior.

Held up by his gratefulness to God and by his wife's challenge, Yesupadam determined to continue in the ministry despite his grief. He decided that he ought to live the rest of his life as a single man, and devote himself even more fully to planting and nurturing churches.

But after a year, other leaders in Visakhapatnam started talking about finding a new wife for Yesupadam. Because of his status in the community, they felt that he ought to be married. "Thank you, my friends," he would say. "But no, I'm not interested in getting married again. I can give more to the ministry as a single man."

Yesupadam politely declined their offers to arrange a marriage for him, but to no avail. They began to invite him over and introduce him to eligible Christian women. After a year of uncomfortable arranged meetings with eligible young women and eager, encouraging matchmakers, things had come to a head. He had to do something. Determined to remain single, Yesupadam was caught up in a dilemma. Christian leaders whom he greatly respected were pressing him to marry, and he couldn't simply disregard their advice. Neither could he shake his own feelings against remarriage. After spending some time in thought, Yesupadam came up with a foolproof solution. He prayed.

"All right, Lord," he said, "I need a clear sign from you if you want me to remarry. If you want me to remarry, send me a white, blonde-haired, blue-eyed woman. And have *her* approach me and ask me to marry her. Otherwise I will remain single."

Satisfied that his prayer would permanently close the door on marriage, Yesupadam was at peace. He threw himself into the ministry, working long hours and traveling extensively. Surrounded by his grown children and his friends and family in the ministry, Yesupadam found comfort and solace after Padmini's death. There were times when he was very lonely, however. After the noise and bustle of the workday, he found it hard to come home to a quiet house and an empty bed.

One night, coming home late, he realized that he had forgotten his keys. He knocked on the door, but everyone was asleep. He knocked again, and again. As he stood there alone on the dark porch in the still of the night, a cold pain gripped his heart, and memories of his life with Padmini rushed back to him.

She used to wait up for me, he thought wistfully. *She knew me so well that she could hear my steps as I walked toward the house. Lord, it's so hard to be without her!*

Despite his loneliness, Yesupadam still didn't feel any desire to remarry. He thought it was easier to endure loneliness than the complications of starting a new family. Besides, Padmini had set such a standard of love and godliness that Yesupadam feared he would never find another woman to live up to her example. He pushed his loneliness aside and continued the work of the ministry.

* * *

Monika's story was very different. She grew up as a German-Canadian farm girl in rural Manitoba—a life worlds away from India. From a young age, however, she knew that God was calling her away from her quiet life. At the age of twelve, while walking to the barn with her mother, she confidently shared that she was going to be a missionary.

But that early faith in God's call was not met with an early answer. Although in Bible college she met others with a strong desire for missions, and their passion fueled Monika's conviction, she didn't seem to feel sent in any particular direction. Some of her friends seemed so sure—they were going to China, to Africa, to South America—but she had none of their self-assurance. It was discouraging to feel so directionless, especially when she longed to be used by God. Struggling with her desire to serve, Monika began crying out to God, asking Him to direct her and send her. Yet He didn't seem to send many answers.

Becoming a missionary wasn't Monika's only unanswered prayer request. She also had a deep, unwavering desire to marry, but she hadn't found anyone that she felt she could live with and work alongside. Fed up with dating, Monika clung to the picture of Isaac and Rebekah. "God," she said. "I'm never dating again. I want you to arrange my marriage. Take me to the man you want me to marry, and show me clearly who he is." But here too, God wasn't providing what she wanted. No husband was in sight. Yet during a time when she had little hope for marriage, she was reminded of a promise expressed by a speaker at a conference she went to. Roy Hessian's words seemed intended directly for her: "God gives his very best to those who leave the choice to Him."

In the midst of this indefinite period of waiting, Monika felt blind. *I want to be going somewhere, doing something, living life with a purpose,* she would think. *But I have no idea what direction to take. Lord, I don't know where you're taking me—or even if you're going to take me anywhere.* It was easy to feel hopeless. To make matters more difficult, she felt outside pressure to "do something" with her life—to settle down, to get married, to move on. But even when she felt like her desires would never be fulfilled, her desire to be used by God, in *His* way, never waned.

And again, just when she was despairing, God would send her encouragers. "I have such hope for your life," her friends and mentors would say. "God is going to use you in a powerful way. Let me be your hope for you."

Monika tried pursuing more education, but God closed the door. She tried to join Youth with a Mission (YWAM), but even though she thought it seemed perfect, and they wanted her to stay, God clearly said no.

Bereft of her dream, Monika found herself doing the only thing she *didn't* want to do—working at a dead-end job, just paying the bills. She felt the farthest away she'd ever felt from her goals, and she was left with only the responsibility of being faithful to the job God had given her.

One day, in August of 1996, one of Monika's friends told her she was going to India for three weeks. The word struck Monika like lightning. *India!* she thought. *India. That's where I need to be.* The thought surged through her whole being. But just as quickly, despairing realism set in. *I can't go. I don't have enough vacation time, or enough money. I need to go long-term, but this group doesn't do long-term.* Frustrated, Monika concluded that she was just trying to make things work on her own again.

But a week later, Monika came home from work to find Yesupadam sitting at the family's dinner table. Al and Paulette, the couple Monika lived with and was mentored by, had heard him speak earlier in the week, and they had invited him to come to their house. As Monika sat down for dinner and listened, she was struck by the Indian man's desire to be led by God. Monika was deeply impressed. She thought, *So many people talk about what they've decided, what they feel. This man talks only about what God shows him, and what God commands him to do.*

When he was done talking about the ministry, Yesupadam looked up at Monika and the other single women at the table. "If you want to come to India," he said. "Come. Come for six months, a year, or longer. You can work with the children and do evangelism with us. If you can only afford a one-way plane ticket, that's fine. Come anyway. We'll take care of you."

It seemed so perfect, but Monika was still nervous, afraid that it would end up as just another dead end. One night, feeling unwell, Monika skipped Bible study and lay in bed praying. "Lord," she said, "I don't know what to do about India. If this isn't from you, I'm not going to think about it ever again. But if it is you, confirm it now."

Opening her Bible, Monika found herself reading Isaiah 55:5:

You will call a nation you do not know,
And a nation which knows you not will run to you,
Because of the Lord your God, even the Holy One of Israel;
For He has glorified you.
(NASB)

The next morning, Monika went downstairs and noticed the Bible study's group prayer journal sitting in the living room. She decided to take a look. When she opened to the notes from the night before, someone had written: "Monika—confirm India." When she saw Paulette afterwards, Paulette said, "Monika, someone gave you ten dollars as seed money for India." It was confirmed. Finally, she had a sense of direction.

Monika sold her car, quit her job, and flew to India on January 25, 1997. She landed on the hot, muggy tarmac in Bombay, and as she climbed out of the plane and felt the humid night air brush her face, she heard a still, small voice say, "You're home."

Soon after she arrived, Yesupadam and the pastors took a group of foreigners on the road for four weeks of evangelism and outreach meetings. As she heard Yesupadam share a few of his responsibilities as Love-n-Care's leader, Monika felt that God wanted her to carry his burdens and pray for him. Three nights later, during an evening crusade meeting, Monika was overtaken by the same burden. Covering her head with her scarf, she began to weep uncontrollably, interceding for Yesupadam's life, praying for God's protection, praying for a wife for him. After an hour and a half, she was able to recover and sit up again. Yesupadam gave an altar call at the end of the message, and then told the foreigners to go out in the crowd and pray for the people. As she walked through the crowd, laying hands on people and praying, Monika turned back to the stage and saw Yesupadam there. Suddenly, she heard an unmistakable voice speak: "He is your husband." Even though the thought seemed humanly ridiculous, Monika had a strange, supernatural peace. She suddenly knew why she had been so burdened for him.

The next morning, everyone packed up to go home and loaded up into vans. Monika ended up being the only foreigner in Yesupadam's van. She began praying for an opportunity to share her news with Yesupadam. Then the tire went flat. Everyone else went back to the nearest town, but Yesupadam and Monika stayed with the van. There was a little hut nearby, and the owners brought out a cot for Monika and Yesupadam to sit on. Seeing an opportunity, Monika didn't waste any time.

"I need to talk to you," she said. "Last night, the Lord spoke to me. He told me that you are going to be my husband." Monika stopped, realizing that she had just put it all on the table, and that there was nothing more for her to say. She waited for his reply, uncomfortable with the silence.

"Let's go sit on the other side of the cot," Yesupadam said, as if nothing had happened. "I want to be able to watch for everyone coming back." So they moved to the other side of the cot. Silence reigned as they watched the empty road.

But after a few long minutes, Yesupadam began to talk. He told Monika about Padmini, about his first marriage, her death, the pressure to remarry, and the ingenious prayer that he had prayed to ensure his singleness. Now, unexpectedly, he was faced with the answer to his prayer.

Yesupadam knew he was trapped by the merciful and ironic hand of God. He had asked the Lord for an impossible request, and here she was, staring him in the face and asking him to marry her. Monika was fair-skinned, green-eyed (but to Indians, all eye colors beside brown are blue), with blondish-brown hair—and she was proposing.

Although it had happened in an instant, Monika and Yesupadam knew that it was settled. After the initial adrenaline rush wore off, however, the weight of it all began to creep in. It took a few months for Yesupadam to settle into the idea that God didn't want him to serve as a single man. For both Monika and Yesupadam, the concept of a cross-cultural and cross-generational marriage was intimidating. In addition, many other people were initially taken aback at the thought of Yesupadam marrying a young white woman whom nobody knew. It was equally hard on Monika's family to learn that their daughter was marrying an Indian man that they'd never met. Yet through the time of transition and testing, their faith in God's provision steadied their resolve to marry.

"I felt very honored that the Lord would choose me for such a high calling—to marry a man like Yesupadam," Monika says. "But there was also a sense of being overwhelmed. Our marriage was definitely something out of the ordinary, something 'unnatural.'

And the unnatural is rarely easy. But the unnatural is worth it in the long run, when it is from the Lord."

A year later, on April 25, 1998, Monika and Yesupadam were married. Convinced that God had called them to serve together and love one another, they embarked on a relationship that bore witness to the unifying power of Christ's love.

Thinking back to his "impossible prayer," Yesupadam is amazed. "I don't pray those prayers anymore," he laughs. "I don't play those games with God. I know Him much better now."

Although Yesupadam knows better than to try to trick God with his crafted prayers, it is clear that God's unexpected answer is a precious and unimaginable gift. Although he didn't think it possible, Yesupadam is again experiencing and returning the love of a faithful, godly wife whose service to God strengthens his own.

Until the Whole World Knows

Ministries like Love-n-Care have redefined the face of modern missions. Despite limited (and often uncertain) resources, the men and women of Love-n-Care have planted churches and proclaimed the Gospel to hundreds of thousands of Indians. Their faithful ministry has made an incalculable difference in southeast India— all without visas, passports, plane tickets, vaccines, cultural immersion techniques, local guides, or bilingual dictionaries. The efficiency and impact of such indigenous missionaries is undeniable. In their effectiveness, native ministries have also redefined the role of the West in missions.

When believers model the Christian life from *within* their unique culture, instead of bringing faith in from the outside, the reality and authority of Christ is on display. It is not as easy to dismiss Christianity as a Western or white religion when those who live it and proclaim it are neither Western nor white! By loving, supporting, funding, and praying for those on the mission field, the churches of the developed world position themselves for maximum effectiveness as well.

Strong indigenous missions provide a meaningful context for foreign involvement. Rather than shutting out the West as imperialist meddlers, local ministries can welcome them for the valuable help that they offer. Those who come to the ministry to teach, preach, provide medical help, and serve on missions trips come alongside local workers and offer valued support. Love-n-Care Ministries has always welcomed those from abroad who come to be involved with their work.

Many westerners who come to Love-n-Care, however, have to adjust some of their original expectations. "Many people who come to serve here arrive with assumptions about what they are here to give," Yesupadam explains. "They need to be taught how to give as true servants, because sometimes what they need to give is different than what they wanted to offer. Our primary goal is to disciple the foreigners who come to work with us—to teach them how to pray, spend time in the Word, and to give them a vision for world missions. We don't make excuses for the downtime foreigners experience here. There is a lot of unscheduled time, which is meant to be used in Bible study and prayer. Sometimes it is hard to teach foreigners these things, and sometimes it doesn't seem worth it. But when you realize all the positive things that they gain from an experience in India, it's definitely worth it."

Some people are surprised to realize that they are primarily viewed as disciples and learners rather than vital and indispensable additions to the ministry. It is important for visitors and friends to realize that they have come not to "fix" the Indian model of ministry, but to contribute to it. Monika has been a great help in navigating these difficult situations. Because she has an understanding of both Eastern and Western cultures and mindsets, she is well-equipped to communicate between visitors and ministry members. Her oversight of the foreign visitors has helped to clarify the rules, expectations, and roles for foreigners at the ministry.

Because those who come to work with Love-n-Care quickly realize that they are there to be discipled as well as to serve, they often come back from their time in India more aware of how they have been changed than of how they have affected India. Learning to pray and to have a burden for world missions are priceless gifts.

This is not to deny, however, the impact that foreigners have had on Love-n-Care Ministries. Those who have answered the call to come and teach or spend time with the children have made an immeasurable contribution to the lives of those young people. With over 200 children at the Children's Home in Visakhapatnam and only a handful of staff members, the children are hungry for more personal time with adults. It is hard to quantify the effect of a smile, a hug, a laugh, or a touched hand in passing, but even the smallest expressions of love towards these children is received with the greatest delight. In those unrushed hours of conversation, fellowship, and play with the children at Bethany, the kingdom of God is being built. The foreigners who have come to work with the children do so much, simply by sharing their love and affection. On the academic side of things, the children learn English much faster as a result of their conversations with Americans, Canadians, and other foreigners who use English to communicate. Since English is one of India's official languages, and the primary business language, such skills are highly coveted.

Outreach events are also made easier with the help of foreigners. "In village outreach," Yesupadam says matter-of-factly, "white people are useful for drawing a crowd." Although it may sound humorous, there is a real benefit in bringing foreigners to the village evangelism missions. There are many places in rural Andhra Pradesh where light-skinned people have never been seen. The pure curiosity factor can draw large crowds in remote villages, which puts them in a position to hear the Gospel. Many people are also affected to hear that those foreigners loved them so much that they would fly halfway around the world just to tell them about Jesus. Since the white people always come with Indian pastors and teachers, they are not afraid of being seen as the bearers of a "foreign" or "Western" Gospel. The curiosity of the villagers is usually only a benefit for those who are preaching.

Foreigners are also helpful in discussions with higher-caste and lighter-skinned Indians. Since "wealthy" white foreigners are considered to be in the highest possible caste, Christians from overseas have instant access to unbelievers who would never talk with a Christian Dalit (untouchable).

Over the last decade or so, Love-n-Care has also benefited greatly from pastors who come from overseas to teach and equip the local pastors and leaders. Many of the pastors and teachers in India are relatively new believers themselves, and most have little or no access to materials on church leadership, doctrine, teaching, or pastoring. In the West, where there is a wealth of exposure to such materials, teaching, and ideas, it is easy to take them for granted. Western Christians are used to pastors with seminary degrees and advanced training. But because of the great need for pastors and the lack of available resources, many Christian pastors in India are sent out with only a Bible and a few physical necessities. Love-n-Care has established the Discipleship Training Center to better equip such pastors, but teachers and leaders from overseas have also helped to fill this need.

"We have a desire to grow in the strength of our teaching," says Yesupadam. "Indians need better teaching and equipping so that they can teach the Word better themselves. It is good to have foreign pastors and teachers come—it's definitely a give-and-take situation. They learn from our strengths here, and we learn from theirs."

With friends from around the world coming to teach and preach at pastors' conferences, DTC classes, and seminars, LNC pastors are increasingly equipped to teach their people from the Word of God with depth, accuracy and zeal. These new strengths are added to their existing ones—faith, perseverance in prayer, humble service, and passionate evangelism.

Financial help has also been one of the West's greatest contributions to Love-n-Care Ministries. Foreigners live surrounded by more wealth than most Indians could ever imagine. And because money stretches much farther in India than it does in most industrialized countries, even modest donations become significant contributions to the ministry. Foreign gifts have helped build churches and homes, sponsor pastors and impoverished children, provide nutritious food for the Children's Home, establish hospitals, furnish medical equipment, supply believers with Bibles, and provide endless other items which strengthen and speed the work of spreading the Gospel.

Although cold, hard cash can sound distressingly unspiritual, it has been the means of funding work that overflows with eternal importance. And there is much more to come. Yesupadam has faith for a host of projects and expansions that many others would be reluctant to hope for. Yet, time and again, he has seen God do more than all he could ask or imagine, and those experiences stir him to believe for more of God's work. "If you are willing to do what God wants you to do," he says, "God will make the way. And the way He leads you is amazing."

Yesupadam's dream of a 100-bed hospital is already past the dreaming and planning stages, and is currently being built. Plans are also being laid to purchase ten to fifteen acres of farmland to help support the dietary needs of the ministry, which are extensive. The ministry serves about 5000 meals a day, which translates into a cost of about $150,000 annually. By growing their own rice and vegetables, and raising their own chickens (for meat and eggs) and cows (for meat and milk), the ministry would be able to save substantial amounts of money, which could be redirected to tribal ministry or other needs. Although the land is expensive—rice fields can cost around $6,000 or $7,000 US per acre—the resulting savings over years would be very cost-effective and so Yesupadam and LNC pray for a farm opportunity.

Prayer is a vital aspect of the ministry, and Yesupadam has plans to build a prayer hall on the mountain where the hospital is to be built. This new "Prayer Mountain" will have a large prayer room for corporate meetings, as well as small individual rooms where intercession can take place 24 hours a day. Yesupadam is passionate about making prayer a round-the-clock ministry at Love-n-Care.

Yesupadam also hopes to help start small businesses in the Christian community, so that more Christians can be self-supportive and have stable incomes. Currently in India, the majority of Christians are in the lowest castes, largely isolating Christianity to poorer areas. As a result, it can be difficult for Indian Christians to reach out to those of higher castes with the Gospel. Establishing Christians in the small business community could change that pattern, and reach more urban and well-to-do families with the good news of Christ's work.

Yesupadam has another project that would seem impossible to many—a university. "I started realizing that we will have a university—JCU, Jesus Cares University, and a Medical College," he says.

It might be easier to send Christians to public universities, but Yesupadam has a different vision for Andhra Pradesh. "Health and education are places where people come to you," as Yesupadam says. "We want to train students and use them as a way to reach the local community with Christianity. We want to impact the educated community in particular. That will change the future of India. The people in India think that Christianity is a poor man's religion. Once more Christians are educated, more communities in India will accept Jesus. We can use that institution as a way to reach people with the Gospel of Jesus Christ. That has been proven in the schools, the junior colleges, the training centers—in every work we've started, that has been true. There is a dire need for educated Christians in this country. I have seen those letters—JCU—and the words "Jesus Cares University" in a vision as I was praying, so I know that it's God's will for us to start it."

It is an exciting thing to realize that God uses willing, listening, faith-filled people in such powerful ways. Even projects like a university that seem elusive or nearly impossible are really no more difficult to God than providing the air that we constantly breathe. As Yesupadam says, "God's ways *are* amazing."

Ultimately, of course, it is the Lord Jesus Christ and not the multitude of opportunities for ministry that is essential. Ministries, goals, efforts, teachings, and financial offerings are nothing without God's blessing and plan. That is why the most important work is done not with our hands, but on our knees. The Lord has promised to come again, and when He does, every race, tribe, and people will worship him. The men and women of Love-n-Care Ministries, as well as those in countless other churches and ministries around the world, are working toward that goal. Although Westerners can support those ministries with time and finances, the most lasting contribution is fervent intercession before the Father for the lost. Paul's exhortation is to "Devote yourselves to prayer, keeping alert in it with an attitude of thanksgiving" (Col. 4:2, NASB). To be faithful in prayer is no easy task, but it is vital to kingdom work. Our prayers are needed for India, China, Russia, Nigeria, Iran, Indonesia, the United States, and countless other nations and people groups. May we be those who persevere and keep alert in prayer, interceding for the nations until they find their joy in Christ!

AFTERWORD

By P. Yesupadam

Dear Friends in Christ Jesus!

What a great God we have. He is El Shaddai, the all-sufficient God, and the God of impossibilities. I was an untouchable poor boy dying with starvation in the middle of the road, but the God who knew me even before the foundations of the world sent a Canadian Baptist missionary all the way across the world to India to pick me up and to help me medically and then financially with my education.

Our God is the beginning and the end, the Alpha and Omega. He sees the end of our lives in their very beginning. I was a no-body, with no address—not respected or even treated as a human being because of my lowest caste and poorest background; but His thoughts and ways are always higher than ours. His plans and purposes are greater than ours. When I was lost in my sins and trespasses as an atheist, communist, and alcoholic gang leader involved in underground activities, a murderer, anti-God, anti-government and anti-affluence, God is his mercy visited me through His only Son Jesus Christ. He not only saved me from my most wretched life but also gave me a mission and purpose for my life, laying Indian people on my heart.

Indians are a very friendly, peace-loving, and religious people. They are searching for God everywhere. They worship 330 million so called gods and goddesses, but millions of them have never even heard the name of Jesus once in their lives. It breaks my heart to see my people slipping away into eternal damnation. The god of this age has blinded the eyes of my people for centuries. Once saved, I was like a crazy man for Jesus on the streets of India, going everywhere I could to meet people with the Gospel, even to the point of risking my own life. The dear Lord has given me such a love and burden for my people.

It is my heart's desire and prayer that as you read this book, the presence and mighty power of God will touch you and grant you a great revelation of who He is and what He can do through the lives of ordinary people like you and me. It's not because of us but because of Him—His love for the world, His glory, and His eternal kingdom purposes. If He can use the brothers and sisters in India mentioned in this book, what would stop Jesus from using you?

It is also my prayer that the heart of God for the salvation of India will be revealed to you. To reach India is to reach one-sixth of the world's population. Thomas the Apostle was the first martyr for the Gospel in India, shedding his blood on our soil. The Bible tells us in Genesis 4:10 that God said to Cain, "The voice of your brother's blood is crying to me from the ground" (NASB). Friends, if the cry of the blood of Abel was heard by God in Heaven, even so the cry of the blood of Thomas is being heard for the nation of India.

The apostle Paul desired to preach where the name of Jesus had never been preached. India is such a place, with millions who have never heard the Good News. While writing to the Ephesian church, Paul poured out his heart, explaining God's purpose for the Church on earth. As he wrote in Ephesians 3:8-11, the Church is to:

1. *Preach the Gospel of the unsearchable riches of Christ to the Gentiles (the unreached).*
2. *Make known the mystery of the Gospel through Jesus Christ which was hidden in God since the beginning of the world.*
3. *Make known the manifold riches of the wisdom of God, even to the principalities and powers in heavenly places.*

Paul called the church at Ephesus to go to the whole world and preach the Gospel of Christ. That word is alive for us today as well. At Love-n-Care Ministries, we are striving to fulfill these commands. We are going to the unreached tribal peoples of India to preach the Gospel to those who have never heard it. We are working to plant churches that will display the "manifold wisdom of God" to believers and a watching world. You can also participate in this as well. Through your support, men and women who were once separated from Christ are being reconciled to God. Through your personal evangelism and heart for missions, you can come and serve alongside your brothers and sisters in India. May God help us in our lives to accomplish God's plan and purpose, by using us to shine in this sin-darkened world.

May the Lord join our hearts and hands together to reach India and the world with the Gospel of Jesus Christ before it is too late. We have only one life...let us invest it into the Kingdom of God. May the Lord richly bless you!

NOTES

[1] Tom O'Neill, "Untouchable," National Geographic, 203 (2003): 2.

[2] Gospel for Asia: Dalit News, "Dalit Christians Equal Rights Case," Gospel for Asia, http://www.gfa.org/indian-court-delays-dalit-christians-equal-rights-case, May 2007.

[3] GFA News, "Court Again Postpones Dalit Decision," Gospel for Asia, http://www.gfa.org/court-again-postpones-dalit-decision.

[4] V. Subramanyam, "Role of Government for the Enhancement of Education Status Among Tribes in the Integrated Tribal Development Agency Area of Paderu, Andhra Pradesh," Studies of Tribes and Tribals , vol. 1, no.3 (December 2003) http://www.krepublishers.com/02-Journals/T%20&%20T/T%20&%20T-01-0-000-000-2003-Web/T%20&%20T-01-2-091-174-2003-Abst-PDF/T%20&%20T-01-2-155-161-2003-Subra/T%20&%20T-01-2-155-161-2003-Subra.pdf.

[5] UNICEF, India: Statistics, http://www.unicef.org/infobycountry/india_india_statistics.html, 2005.

[6] Sebastiao Salgado, India, http://www.endofpolio.org/countries/india.html, 2005.

[7] Global Polio Eradication Initiative, The Disease and Virus, http://www.polioeradication.org/disease.asp, 2005.

[8] Ministry of Health and Family Welfare, National Health Policy, section 2.4.1, "The State of Public Health Infrastructure," http://mohfw.nic.in/np2002.htm, 2002.

CONTACT INFORMATION

For more information about Love-n-Care Ministries, a subscription to the weekly e-newsletter, or to learn more about getting involved:

Visit the website at:

www.love-n-careministries.org

Or contact the ministry via email at:

mail@love-n-careministries.org

Or send mail to:

**Love-n-Care Ministries USA
P.O. Box 535
North Bennington, VT 05257-0535**

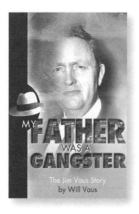

Will Vaus

MY FATHER WAS A GANGSTER
The Jim Vaus Story

One of the most fascinating conversion stories of the 20th century—the dramatic life story of Jim Vaus, former associate to America's underworld.

Mary Haskett

REVEREND MOTHER'S DAUGHTER
A Real Life Story

In this gripping account, the author shares her personal story of racial rejection, physical and sexual abuse, and wartime trauma. Through it all, she is aware of a driving force in her life that ultimately brings her to Jesus Christ.

Fanny Goose
with Janet Fridman

RISING FROM THE HOLOCAUST
The Life of Fanny Goose

The astonishing real life story of an indomitable young Jewish girl who miraculously survives the horrors of Hitler's plot to destroy her people and goes on to live a joyful life.

www.BelieveBooks.com

Also available from Believe Books:

Major General Jerry R. Curry

FROM PRIVATE TO GENERAL
*An African American Soldier
Rises Through the Ranks*

Major General Jerry Curry vividly describes
his life journey of military missions, powerful positions, and his relationship with
the true source of authority—his Father in
heaven.

Charlene Curry

THE GENERAL'S LADY
God's Faithfulness to a Military Spouse

Charlene Curry recounts all the joys and
challenges of being a career military spouse
and how she triumphed over difficulties by
relying on a source of spiritual power that
transformed her life.

Fern C. Willner

WHEN FAITH IS ENOUGH
*A Safari of Destiny that Reveals
Principles to Live By*

A faith-inspiring story of a missionary
wife and mother of seven relying completely on God in the heart of Africa.

Harvey Katz

BECOMING A GOD MAGNET
The Secret to Sharing Your Faith
Book and **Study & Discussion Guide**

Harvey Katz's book *Becoming a God Magnet* is a practical, effective guide to evangelism. The *Study & Discussion Guide* is ideal for church or home groups willing to learn and share successful methods of personal evangelism.

Howard Katz

SEVEN ESSENTIAL RELATIONSHIPS
How To Pass God's Crucial Tests

The author uses the seven stages in the creation of a clay vessel, as well as an exposition of the life of Joseph, to illustrate each of the seven crucial tests that every believer must pass.

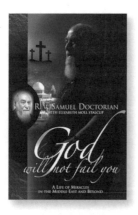

Rev. Samuel Doctorian
with Elizabeth Moll Stalcup, Ph.D.

GOD WILL NOT FAIL YOU
A Life of Miracles in the Middle East and Beyond

The miraculous life story of Rev. Samuel Doctorian, the renowned evangelist used mightily by God in the Middle East and around the world.